Growing Up In the Shadow of the Great Depression

The Early Life of Jean Berthiaume

Growing Up

In the Shadow of

The Great Depression

The Early Life of Jean Berthiaume

Barbara Dube Costa

First Printing 2014
ISBN-10: 1499145705
ISBN-13: 9781499145700
paulandbarbc@cox.net

Dedicated to my mother, Jeannette "Jean" Berthiaume Dube. Although she faced many obstacles in her young life, she overcame them and became stronger and more resourceful because of them. She taught me how our family and life experiences mold and shape us into the person we become.

Introduction

Although this is a book of fiction, it is based on recollections told to me by my mother. It is written in the context of the times and historical events that shaped her life. The headlines at the beginning of each chapter appeared in the *Fall River Herald News* newspapers of that year. They are included in order to give the reader some perspective on the times in which Jean grew up.

Jean was born and raised in Fall River, Massachusetts. When she left, she was a young married woman with one child and another on the way. It was 1941. The United States would soon be at war, another defining event for her generation, just as the Great Depression defined her childhood. She did not return to Fall River to live until she was eighty-two and a widow. She died in Fall River at the age of ninety-one while still living independently. Jean often marveled that she and all her sisters lived into their nineties though her father and mother died so young.

HEADLINES OF THE TIMES

THE FALL RIVER HERALD NEWS
1919

PEACE TREATY FORMALLY SIGNED AT.VERSAILLES

SENATE APPROVES WOMEN'S SUFFRAGE ACT
ORIGINALLY DRAFTED BY SUSAN B. ANTHONY

AL JOLSEN SINGS BIGGEST HIT "ON THE ROAD TO
CALAIS"

NEW LABOR LAW FOR CHILDREN UNDER 14

CITY EMPLOYEES' UNION OUT ON STRIKE

RED SOX TAKE DOUBLE-HEADER FROM NEW YORK

BABE RUTH HITS 25TH HOMER OF SEASON

SUPREME COMMANDER OF EXPEDITIONARY FORCES
GEN. PERSHING CHEERED AS HE LANDS ON U.S. SOIL

TEXTILE WORKERS VOTE TO STRIKE

CALVIN COOLIDGE REELECTED GOV. OF MASS.

RI BEGINS.COURT CHALLENGE OF PROHIBITION LAW

GREAT BOOTLEGGER ROUNDUP PLANNED BY GOV'T

STEEL MAGNATE ANDREW CARNEGIE DIES

1919

Nineteen hundred and nineteen was an eventful year. World War I – the "Great War to End All Wars" – had finally ended. The peace treaty was signed in Versailles. General Pershing, Supreme Commander of the American Expeditionary Forces, received rousing ovations when he returned to the United States. Prohibition became the law of the land when the Volstead Act was passed by congress. The U.S. Senate approved the Women's Suffrage act originally drafted by Susan B. Anthony and first introduced to the senate in 1878. Calvin Coolidge was reelected Governor of Massachusetts. The interests of the American people returned once more to the daily struggles of the working class. Labor unions were rising up against pitifully low wages and horrible working conditions. The City Employees Union, for the first time in Fall River history, went out on strike. A steel workers strike began in Pittsburg and spread across the country. Textile workers in Fall River voted to strike. The strike spread to New Bedford and across New England. It eventually became the biggest strike in the history of the textile industry. A coal miners' strike led to a shortage of coal and caused the shut-down of many cotton mills. And amid all these events, ordinary people went about their daily lives growing up, getting married, having families, and working to support them.

In the early nineteen hundreds, Fall River was a bustling industrial city popularly known as "Spindle City" because of its many cotton textile mills. Immigrants from many countries were drawn there by the plentiful jobs in the mills. Most of the French immigrants coming from Canada had settled in their own neighborhoods. One of these was known as "the Flint". They gathered together to share their common language, customs, and religious practices. Almost all of those living "up the Flint" belonged to Notre Dame d'Lourdes (Roman Catholic) Church and attended Mass officiated by French speaking priests. These families sent their children to catholic schools which were taught by French nuns. The neighborhood provided a sense of belonging for the many French Canadians living there and neighbors tended to form close bonds with each other. Most families spoke French in the home because they wanted their children to continue their French customs and heritage. There were several French language newspapers published in Fall River at that time. The most prominent one was called L'Independent.

Memé (Jean's grandmother) was born and raised in Quebec, Canada. She came to the United States as a young women and married, Peter Rioux. They had three daughters and three sons. Rosanna (Jean's mother) was the oldest. She was born in Fall River in 1891. When Memé became a young widow she took Rosanna and the other children back to Quebec. She eventually married Delphis Guay and had two more daughters and two sons. They all returned to Fall River, Massachusetts when Roseanna was in her late teens.

When Roseanna was nineteen, she married James Berthiaume (November 30, 1912) who was ten years older than she. Together they started a family. Jeannette "Jean" was born on June 23, 1919. She was the youngest of four daughters. Bernadette was six, Anita was four, and Lillian was three at that time. James died when Jean was still a baby. They all lived on the second floor of a three story tenement up the Flint in Fall River. Rosanna's brother Alcide and his wife Germaine lived upstairs on the third floor. Memé, Rosanna's sister Florida, her husband Wilfred and their five children lived on the first floor. Three other tenements surrounded the small dirt yard. They were mostly occupied by extended family.

HEADLINES OF THE TIMES

THE FALL RIVER HERALD NEWS
1924

HEAVYWEIGHT CHAMP DEMPSEY TO FIGHT
GIBBONS

SOVIET PREMIER LENIN DIES

SERIOUS FIRE IN MARSHALL'S HAT FACTORY

FORMER PRESIDENT WOODROW WILSON DIES

KLANSMEN BATTLE SHERIFF IN "BOOTLEG WAR"

FORMER PRESIDENT WOODROW WILSON DIES

PRICES FOR FOOD ARE TOO HIGH

UNITED TEXTILE WORKERS TO FIGHT ANY
PAY CUT

FLINT MILL WEAVERS VOTE TO STRIKE

GUN FIGHT IN RUM RAID

NEW TUBERCULOSIS HOSPITAL READY FOR
PATIENTS

NOTRE DAME D'LOURDES CHURCH CELEBRATES
GOLDEN JUBILEE

REELECTION SWEEP FOR PRESIDENT COOLIDGE

1924

Momma sat in her rocking chair mending socks. Her fingers moved deftly, weaving the thread in and out as she darned. Five year old Jeannette was in the swing Momma had hung in the doorway. Her little feet barely touched the floor. Momma had begun calling Jeannette "Jean" and soon everyone was calling her Jean too. Outside, the yard was warm and pleasant as the sun beat down on the packed dirt. It was ringed by three tenement houses, each rising three stories above the playing children. Nita and Lil used a stick they found to draw squares for a game of hopscotch. The air was heavy with dust being kicked up from the children's feet.

Two boys from the neighborhood came sauntering up to where Bernie was playing marbles. She flicked the shooter with her thumb and knocked two marbles out of the circle she had drawn in the dirt. "Hey Bernie, bet I can beat you," she heard. Bernie looked up at the boys standing nearby. Jacky reached into his pants pocket. "Aw shucks! That's the one with the hole in it," he said. His pants were dirty and baggy. His shirt hung over his belt half in and half out. His cap was tilted over his left eye. He figured he could take any girl at this game. His younger brother Joey stood next to him tugging at his socks as they kept sliding down around his ankles. Jacky reached into his other pocket and pulled out a handful of marbles. Then he pulled out a shooter from his shirt pocket. Bernie stood up, her dress falling unevenly below her knees. "Who says," she dared him. She was not one to back down from a challenge, especially from a smart-aleck boy like Jacky.

The three huddled around the circle drawn in the dirt and tossed their marbles inside its boundaries. "Oldest goes first," announced Jacky with a smirk. Then he took his shooter and placed it between his forefinger and thumb. He flicked his thumb and the shooter blasted into the circle, knocking five marbles out. He picked up the ousted marbles, shoved them in his pocket and slowly moved around the circle. He flicked his shooter again with his thumb. This time three marbles flew out of the circle. He grabbed them and shot again, all the time bragging about how he would win all the marbles in the circle. Bernie studied him with piercing eyes. Jacky shot again. The marbles bounced against each other but stayed inside the circle.

Bernie took her cue. She slowly rounded the circle then stooped down and flicked her shooter as hard as she could. It bounced off a cluster of marbles. They scattered and bounced against each other forcing the four outer ones over the edge of the circle. She grabbed them and placed them in her cloth bag. She glared at Jacky who tried to look nonchalant. Bernie shot again. Three more marbles bounced out. Her next shot slipped from her finger and rolled slowly against the marbles still in the circle. They shuffled around but stayed within the line. Jacky looked at her with a sarcastic grin. Joey looked nervous. He never can beat his brother but maybe he can beat a girl. He placed his shooter between his finger and thumb. He flicked his thumb awkwardly and the shooter rolled out into the circle without touching any marbles. Joey grabbed his shooter and stuffed it in his pocket with disgust. He looked up at Jacky who just glared at him. Jacky pulled out his shooter again. He walked around the circle confidently, and so it went until there were only three marbles left in the circle. Joey was out of the game by now, his little hands unable to control his shooter effectively. Jacky said to Bernie, "You'll never make it. I can get those three in one shot!" Bernie returned his stare but said nothing. Bragging is for losers she thought to herself. She circled the ring. She aimed her shooter and flicked it with her thumb forcefully. It rolled into the circle and hit the nearest marble. That marble flew into the next one and bounced off the third one. The momentum of the strikes forced the three marbles outside of the circle. Bernie picked up her shooter and the three marbles then walked up to Jackie defiantly. He yelled, "You cheated," grabbed his brother by his collar and stomped off.

HEADLINES OF THE TIMES

THE FALL RIVER HERALD NEWS

1925

MILLS CUT WAGES TEN PERCENT

MINUMUM WAGE OF $6 A DAY SOUGHT

EARTH QUAKE TREMORS TERRIFY NORTH END
PEOPLE

PRES. COOLIDGE'S INAUGURAL SPEECH HEARD
OVER RADIO

NOT ONE TYPHOID FEVER DEATH IN FALL RIVER

FALL RIVER WINS U.S. SOCCER TITLE

LINDBERGH FLIES ACROSS ATLANTIC FROM NEW
YORK TO PARIS

COAST GUARDSMAN SHOT BY RUM RUNNERS

ARCTIC EXPLORER AMUNDSEN FOUND SAFE;
MISSES NORTH POLE BY 120 MILES

GRAND JURY INDICTS SCOPES FOR TEACHING
EVOLUTION
WILLIAM JENNINGS BRYAN PROSECUTOR ;
CLARENCE DARROW DEFENSE

FIRESTONE TIRE & RUBBER TO EXPAND MILL

SCOPES FOUND GUILTY AS LAWYERS QUIT
IN DISGUST

1925

Momma was hard at work cleaning and washing out clothes. When she was done, she picked up a little dress to mend. She tried to sew the skirt to the waistband where it was pulled apart, but the fabric was so worn out that the stitches wouldn't hold. She held the pieces in her hands and thought, "What's the use. Maybe my sister Florida would have a dress that doesn't fit her girls anymore."

It was getting to be lunch time. She rummaged around looking for something to feed the children. There were a few slices of bread left and a jar of molasses. It would have to do. The flat was cold. There was no coal left to heat up the room. The furniture, what little there was, was old and worn out. There were no rugs for the floors. It was very hard to manage since Poppa had died and she was left alone to raise her four daughters.

Momma reached for the jar she kept on a shelf over the sink. There was a nickel inside. She called Bernie in and gave it to her. She told her to go down to the corner and see if the fruit peddler was there so she could buy some bananas. Bernie headed out and as she hurried through the yard, Jean asked if she could go with her. Jean liked to go places with her big sister Bernie. Whenever the neighborhood boys would tease her by calling her names, she would threaten to tell Bernie on them. They would always back off ever since Bernie beat up Billy for pulling her sister Nita's hair. Bernie was a tomboy and she wasn't afraid of any of them.

Bernie let Jean come with her. When they got to the corner they saw "Old Man" Lebeau standing next to his horse-drawn produce cart. Bernie approached, running her hand along the horse's flank as she passed. She and "Tobey" were old friends. He snorted and tossed his head in recognition. "Have you got any bananas today Mr. Lebeau?" she asked. He grabbed his suspenders and snapped them against his chest. "Hey, how's my favorite big sis today," he said, "and your kid sister taggin' along. Course I got bananas." There was a loud noise from across the street and the horse startled, causing the cart to roll back a few inches. "Whoa Tobey, don't get spooked now," said Mr. Lebeau. Jean jumped away from the horse and moved closer to Bernie. "Don't be scared Jean. Tobey won't hurt you," Bernie reassured her. Mr. Lebeau smiled at Bernie. She reminded him of his oldest girl, always looking out for her younger sisters.

"Momma found us a nickel and she wants some bananas. How many can I get for a nickel?" asked Bernie. "Well, let me see now, they're a nickel a bunch," the old man answered. Jean grabbed a small bunch near the edge of the cart but Mr. Lebeau grabbed them from her. "Aw, that's not enough for all of you Berthiaume girls and your Momma. Take this one," and he handed a bigger bunch to Bernie with a little wink, "and you can save your nickel for next time." "Thanks Mr. Lebeau," said Bernie as she clutched the bananas and grabbed Jean's hand.

When they got home, Momma had spread molasses on their bread and poured what was left of the milk in each of four glasses for her daughters. The bananas were a special treat and they saved them for supper.

———————

Momma married Arthur Pelletier, who was also widowed, when Jean was six years old. Arthur had two brothers and two sisters who also lived in Fall River, and a daughter from his first wife. His daughter lived with her grandmother. They often got together with their families and the girls got to know their new cousins.

One day Momma was busy packing sandwiches and fruit to take for a picnic at the summer camp on South Watuppa Pond. The camp belonged to Arthur's family. Jean was all excited. She loved going to the camp. She ran around helping Momma gather jackets and hats to take along. Uncle Alcide and Aunt Germaine came in with some games for the children to play with. When everybody was ready, they all squeezed into Uncle Alcide's automobile. He was the only one in the family who had one and he enjoyed taking everyone out in it. They drove slowly down through the dusty streets dodging horse-drawn wagons, trucks and other automobiles. It was a warm breezy Saturday morning and everyone was out peddling goods, going in and out of stores or standing around chatting with neighbors and acquaintances.

When they got away from the main streets of the city, the roads became less congested. There were trees and grassy areas along the way. After a while, the

Watuppa Pond came slowly into view. It was a large pond surrounded by little cabins, outhouses and small boats pulled up along the shore. As they approached the boat landing at the north end of the pond, they could see a number of other people waiting. Uncle Alcide parked the car and everyone unloaded their belongings. The motor launch that ferried people to their summer camps arrived at the landing. Everyone got aboard with their lunch baskets, fishing gear and supplies. It was just a short distance to the Pelletiers' camp. When they arrived, Arthur stepped out of the launch and helped the others disembark. They all headed up the hill to the cabin carrying their belongings. The cabin was small and cozy. It was a rustic two room wooden cabin painted barn red and had a black asphalt roof. There was a small wood-burning stove used for cooking in the main room, a long wooden table with benches in the middle of the room and a large bed in the corner. There was also a long couch against the side wall and an ice box for food. In the other room there were several mattresses for the children to sleep on. Everyone who stayed there was expected to clean it up before they left for home. There was an outhouse next to it – not a place to linger. Some of Arthur's relatives would take turns staying there for a few days at a time but Arthur never wanted to go for more than a day at a time. Jean liked to go there because she could play in the water with her sisters and the other children from the camp. It was like a vacation.

In the back of the cabin, the ground sloped down to the edge of the pond. At night, you could look around the pond and see lights from the other cabins which surrounded it. When the wind was right you would see tiny sailboats gliding along and people in row boats with their fishing poles hanging over the sides in hopeful expectation. The four sisters rolled up their overalls and walked down to the water. There was a large maple tree at the edge of the pond that had gone down in a wind storm earlier in the summer. Most of it extended out into the water. Bernie climbed up and walked along the trunk. Her sisters hesitated to follow her but she called to them as she dangled from one of the large branches. Nita said she wasn't about to go but Lil started across the trunk. Jean looked at Nita, then the tree and decided she'd stay put. Lil slid one foot after the other along the trunk until she was half way to Bernie, then her foot hit a wet spot and she slipped. Before she knew it, she slid into the water. She began to scream but Bernie told her to be quiet and grab a branch. She was afraid Momma would hear her and make them stay in the cabin.

Bernie moved along the tree trunk, grabbing branches along the way. Lil was beginning to panic as she splashed around in the water. Bernie held on to a branch and reached out to Lil. Grabbing the strap of her overalls, she pulled her up until she was able to wrap her leg around the tree trunk and raise herself up. Bernie laughed and said she looked like a drowned rat with her curly blonde hair and clothes all wet. She heard Momma talking to her friend in the next cabin but she couldn't see her. She said, "Come on Lil, let's get out of here and hide in the bushes until you dry off." Bernie grabbed Jean and Nita and pulled them along as she and Lil ran to hide. When they were safely hidden behind the bushes, they all started to giggle.

16

HEADLINES OF THE TIMES

THE FALL RIVER HERALD NEWS

1926

CARDINAL O'CONNELL OPPOSES PROHIBITION

ALIENS IN NEW ENGLAND FACE DEPORTATION

BUILDING BLOWN TO SPLINTERS IN BOOT-
LEGGERS FEUD

25 INFLUENZA CASES; THREE DEATHS RESULT

SEEK 8 HOUR DAY AND 70¢ AN HOUR WAGES

LT.CMDR. BYRD FIRST TO FLY OVER NORTH POLE

STUDENT AT NOTRE DAME PAROCHIAL SCHOOL
COMPETES IN NATIONAL SPELLING BEE

RUDOLPH VALENTINO DIES OF INFECTION
AFTER SURGERY

3 STORY BUILDING TOPPLES ON SOUTH MAIN ST.

REPORT HEALTHY CONDITIONS IN CLOTH MARKET

FIRE BREAKS OUT IN ST. JOSEPH'S ORPHANAGE;
NUNS LEAD 550 CHILDREN TO SAFETY

"FIGHTING MARINE" GENE TUNNEY WINS WORLD
BOXING CHAMPIONSHIP

1926

Momma was busy in the kitchen getting breakfast ready. Arthur grabbed his lunch pail and headed off to work as soon as he was done eating. Bernie was the first one up when Momma called out to them. She told her sisters that they had better get up and dressed or they would be late for school.

They all got dressed and hurried to the kitchen for breakfast. Momma smiled and told them she had something to tell them. They all sat at the table. Momma filled their bowls with oatmeal and gave each of them a piece of toast and a glass of milk. Bernie asked Momma what she wanted to tell them. "Well," she said, "pretty soon we'll have a new baby." The girls got all excited. "When Momma? When?" begged Jean. "In a couple of months," she said. "Will we be able to play with her?" Jean asked. "You can all help me take care of her – or maybe it will be a boy," she answered. "I'll be able to feed her and take her for walks won't I Momma?" asked Bernie. "Sure," said Momma, "now you all need to get going to school." The four sisters started talking about all the things they would do with the baby as they hurried off to school.

Every week they asked Momma when the baby was coming and every week she said, "Not yet." Finally it was time to get ready for the new arrival. Momma borrowed a crib from Aunt Florida. She set it up in the kitchen because it was the warmest room in the tenement. She went into her bedroom with the girls following her every move. They had been waiting eagerly for signs of the approaching time. Momma opened the large chest and they all dove in, pulling out baby clothes that had been carefully stored away. One by one, they sorted the various items. Some had been used for them when they were babies and some were passed along from their cousins. "Momma, do you think it will be a boy or a girl?" Jean asked excitedly. "It's time we had a boy in the family," announced Bernie. Nita said she thought it would be a girl because boys are so much trouble. Lil said it didn't matter to her. "It will be fun just having a baby to play with," she said.

After they chose the clothes they wanted, they stacked them neatly in piles and placed them in the bureau drawer that Momma had emptied out. Then they folded and stacked the diapers on top. "What are we going to call the baby?" asked Jean. Everyone started saying all the names they liked and Momma made two lists – one for girls' names and one for boys. Then they started voting for their favorites. For boys it was Peter, Normand and Joseph and for girls it was Theresa, Angela and Suzanne. Momma smiled and said she liked them all but her favorites were Robert and Germaine.

For the rest of the day, the four sisters talked about the things they would do with the baby and how much fun it would be. Momma and Aunt Florida carried a box of baby toys upstairs and the girls looked through them. Bernie drew a huge calendar on a piece of paper and circled the day the baby was due. "Three more weeks," she announced. For the next three weeks they marked off each day but the baby didn't come. Finally, the big day came – five days late. Momma told Arthur to ask Memé to call the midwife.   When the girls got home from school the bedroom door was closed. Arthur was pacing the floor in the kitchen. Memé and Aunt Florida were going in and out of the bedroom and telling the children to be quiet so Momma could rest. They heard occasional moans coming from the bedroom. It seemed to go on forever.

Finally they heard a loud cry, a moan and then a baby cry. After a few minutes, Memé came out smiling and said it was a boy. Arthur looked drained but he finally relaxed and breathed a sigh of relief. A little while later, the midwife brought the baby out for them to see. He was all wrapped up in a blanket. The girls marveled at how tiny he was. Aunt Florida told them not to touch him too much so he wouldn't get their germs. The baby was named Robert.

All the toys were lined up like cars on a train. There was a wooden horse with wheels and a pull cord. There was a little doll made out of cloth. There were ten wooden blocks and a baby rattle. Jean picked up the rattle and brought it to Robert. She was fascinated by how tiny he was. She loved to wrap his little fingers around hers. He would try to squeeze her finger, and then he would kick his tiny feet and laugh. This delighted Jean no end. "Momma, can I hold him?" she asked. Momma told her to sit in a chair and she laid Robert in her lap. "Now don't let him go Jean. You have to keep holding on to him like I showed you," Momma warned. "Yes, Momma. I won't let go," Jean assured her as she cuddled her baby brother. "Can we take him for a walk this afternoon Momma?" she asked. Momma said she had a lot of work to do but she could take him out in the carriage if Bernie was with her. Jean cooed and laughed with little Robert until he finally got tired and began to cry. She carefully carried him to his crib and laid him down for a nap.

When Bernie came in from playing outside, Jean asked her if she would take a walk with her and the baby. Bernie was thirteen and loved to play the big sister role. She told Jean they would go after lunch. Momma had made some French pea soup from a ham bone with a few scraps of meat on it that she got at the market. She called Nita and Lil in and they all ate the soup. As they ate, Nita and Lil chattered away about playing jump rope and hop scotch with their friends this morning. After checking with Momma, Bernie announced that she and Jean were taking Robert for a walk to Lafayette Park if anyone else wanted to come. Lil and Nita said they wanted to go. Momma got out the carriage and Bernie got little Robert ready to go out. She carried him to the carriage and gently placed him in it, wrapping a blanket around him to keep him warm. Momma told Bernie not to stay too long at the park and they all left as she resumed her housework. Bernie let her sisters take turns pushing the carriage. As they went along, they waved to the neighbors and stopped to let them admire little Robert. He loved being outdoors and smiled at everyone. The sidewalk was crowded with pedestrians on this warm and breezy spring day. When they got to the park, Jean and Bernie sat on one of the benches, placing the carriage in front of them so that they could see the baby. Lil and Nita went over to the swings. As they rode on the swings, they talked to each other in French.

Two young boys came sauntering over to the swings as they kicked a can back and forth between them. The bigger boy looked about twelve years old. He had reddish hair and freckles. His friend was about the same age but not as tall. He had brown hair, fair complexion and a noticeable lisp. One of the boys said to Nita, "Hey Frenchie, you ought to go back to Canada. You don't belong here." The other boy grabbed the swing Lil was riding on and pulled it to a stop. Lil stayed on the swing and tried to kick him, but he jumped back and let go. Bernie had been watching from the bench and when she saw the boy grab Lil's swing, she stood up and headed toward them. The boys didn't notice her until she was standing behind Lil. "Maybe you should go find some boys to pick on," Bernie said while looking straight at the boy who had grabbed Lil's swing. Bernie was taller and a bit heavier than the boy. She walked around Lil and stood in front of him with her hands on her hips. She stared directly at him. As he stepped back, she stepped forward. The other boy walked over to his friend and said, "Let's go," as he grabbed his arm. They both backed away as Bernie stared them down. Finally, they both turned around and headed away from the swings. As Bernie walked back to the bench, Lil and Nita went back to swinging.

Another boy had been watching from a short distance. He walked over to Bernie and said, "Hi Bernie." She said, "Hi Alfred. I didn't see you there. I watched you

22

playing soccer Saturday, but I had to leave early. Did your team win the game?" Alfred was fourteen and Bernie thought he was very handsome. She smiled and he smiled back. "Yah, we beat them five to two. It was an easy win." Alfred knew Bernie from school and he admired her lack of fear toward boys. Bernie introduced him to Jean. Alfred slid onto the bench and started talking to Bernie. When it was time to go, Alfred offered to walk them home. Bernie said, "Sure. That would be nice of you. I like your company." Once again, she gave him a broad smile and once again, he smiled back. Bernie called for Nita and Lil and they all walked back home together. Jean was pushing the carriage and Robert was shaking his rattle and kicking his little feet.

HEADLINES OF THE TIMES

THE FALL RIVER HERALD NEWS

1927

ANOTHER ENCOURAGING WEEK IN CLOTH MARKET;
MILL OUTLOOK BRIGHTER THAN IN PAST TWO YEARS

SACCO &VANCETTI MURDER CASE REOPENED

FEDERAL RAIDERS GET BIG LIQUOR HAUL ON FALL
RIVER LINE WHARF

HENRY FORD RECOVERING FROM SEVERE ACCIDENT

LINBERGH CHEATS DEATH FLYING NIGHT MAIL

LIZZIE BORDEN DEAD AT SEVENTY-SIX

CHAMBERLIN'S STUNT FLYING THRILLS BERLINERS

ARMY FLYERS MAKE HONOLULU SAFELY; SET NEW
RECORD FOR FLIGHT OF 2400 MILES OVER WATER

BYRD DESCRIBES TERROR OF FLYING IN STORM
OVER FRANCE

SACCO & VANCETTI EXECUTED IN ELECTRIC CHAIR

BOXING CHAMP TUNNEY DEFEATS DEMPSEY FOR
SECOND TIME

PRESIDENT COOLIDGE ELIMINATES HIMSELF AS
CANDIDATE FOR REELECTION

FALL RIVER FAST BECOMING MAJOR PORT

1927

Momma was in the kitchen baking bread. Jean was sitting on the floor playing with Robert and keeping warm by the stove. She had a ball that she rolled on the floor toward Robert. He picked it up and held it in his little hands, and then he threw it on the floor. It rolled over to Jean and Robert laughed, then he started coughing. He coughed for several minutes, unable to stop. Momma picked him up and felt his forehead. She said he felt hot and she thought he had a fever. She gave him some cough syrup made with honey, and then she sat in the rocking chair near the stove. She rocked him until he quieted down and stopped coughing. There was a lot of talk among the neighbors about a whooping cough epidemic and Momma was worried.

During the night, Robert woke up coughing several times and Momma would rock him back to sleep each time. By morning, she noticed that he was making a whooping sound as he tried to catch his breath between coughing spells. Memé came up stairs to see how he was doing. When she heard him coughing, she said it was time to see Doctor Violette.

Doctor Violette was a young man who had opened an office on Eastern Avenue. He was a typical neighborhood physician who made house calls and delivered babies in the home. Everyone up the Flint knew him. They could go to see him in his office without an appointment. He ran the office by himself. He had no staff and never sent out any bills. His patients paid what they could, when they could. Unfortunately, in those days there weren't a lot of medicines to treat illnesses, mainly aspirin for fevers, morphine for pain, and digitalis for heart ailments. There were no lab tests either. Periodically there would be epidemics of polio, measles, whooping cough, scarlet fever, and diphtheria. These illnesses caused the death of many young children.

When Arthur came home from work, Momma wrapped Robert in a blanket and Arthur carried him up Pleasant Street, all the way to Eastern Avenue and Doctor Violette's office. The doctor saw him right away. Robert began to cry when Arthur unwrapped him and Doctor Violette started examining him. Robert started coughing. Doctor Violette knew right away that he had whooping cough. He prescribed a cough syrup and aspirin for his fever. He told Arthur to give him as much fluids as possible and keep him out of drafts.

During the next two weeks, Momma gave him the medicine Doctor Violette had prescribed. Bernie and Momma took turns rocking him when he had a coughing spell. They gave him extra bottles of milk and water as much as he would take. For a while, he seemed to be getting better, but by the third week he looked pale and listless. He was coughing almost constantly and making that whooping sound. Momma and Arthur were very worried. Finally Momma called Doctor Violette on the telephone and asked him to come and see Robert. Doctor Violette came later that afternoon. After examining Robert, he told Momma and Arthur that there was an epidemic of whooping cough around the city. He was very sorry but there was nothing more he could do. Momma began to cry and Arthur put his arms around her, trying to console her. The doctor gave her another bottle of cough syrup and told her to keep giving him the aspirin every four hours to keep his fever down.

Another week went by. Memé came upstairs to help Momma. Together, they would sponge Robert down when his fever went up. They tried to give him milk and water in a bottle but most of the time he wouldn't take it. Bernie would rock him when she got home from school to give Momma a break. Momma was exhausted and beside herself with worry. Finally one night she fell asleep and didn't wake up until early morning. She got up and went to check on Robert. She hadn't heard him coughing and thought he must be getting better at last. She looked at him lying in his crib. When he didn't move, she put her hand on his little back. He felt cold. She rolled him over and began to scream. Arthur woke up and ran to her side. She looked like she was ready to collapse. Robert had not moved. He had not taken a breath. His little body was cold and lifeless. The four sisters came into the room. They looked at Momma and each began to cry and wrap their arms around each other. There were many grieving families as the epidemic swept through the city.

HEADLINES OF THE TIMES

THE FALL RIVER HERALD NEWS
1928

BUILDING OF MOUNT HOPE BRIDGE BEGINS

GALE CAUSES EXTENSIVE DAMAGE TO MILLS;
ISLAND PARK ROLLER COASTER SMASHED TO BITS

CENTER OF CITY SWEPT BY DEVASTATING FIRE;
36 BUILDINGS LEVELED IN 8 HOURS; 250 INJURED

BIG RUM RAIDS IN WESTPORT AND TIVERTON

REPUBLICANS NOMINATE HOOVER FOR PRESIDENT

GOV. AL SMITH CHOSEN DEMOCRATIC CANDIDATE

HOOVER VICTORY OVERWHELMING

AMELIA EARHART 1ST WOMAN TO FLY ATLANTIC

FALL RIVER LAD EUGENE BELISLE OARSMAN IN
OLYMPIC GAMES

HUNDREDS OF PICKETERS ARRESTED IN NEAR RIOT
IN NEW BEDFORD TEXTILE STRIKE

STATE POLICE RAID GAMBLING DEN AT SAWDY POND

GERMAN DIRIGIBLE GRAF ZEPPELIN FLIES OVER U. S.
CAPITAL; PARADE PLANNED IN NEW YORK

ARKWRIGHT MILL BOUGHT BY HOMER LORING –
FIRST STEP IN REHAB OF LOCAL TEXTILE INDUSTRY

1928

Record low temperatures held the city of Fall River in an icy grip. The wind was blowing fiercely. Darkness was descending on the streets as people hurried home from a long day's work. Suddenly a siren began to scream in the dark and within minutes fire sirens could be heard all over the city. The fire started in the Pocasset Mill in the south end known as "the Globe". The building had been empty for several years and all the machinery had been removed. Workers had already removed the water sprinklers and had started to break down walls as they dismantled the mill. No one knows exactly how the fire started, but after decades of soaking up oil from the spinning mules and looms of the textile mill, the wooden floors caught fire quickly. The wind-driven flames spread through the mill uncontrollably. By the time the firemen and fire apparatus arrived, the mill was completely engulfed in flames. The strong winds carried the flames and embers to adjacent buildings. Soon an entire block was burning. The fire continued to spread first in one direction, then as the wind shifted, it went in another direction. Firemen struggled with freezing hoses as they tried to drown the flames. Icicles formed on everything as the temperature dropped. Buildings all along South Main Street, as far as North Main Street and many side streets in either direction, began burning. Fortunately, the fire had started after business hours, so many of the buildings had few occupants; however, the two downtown movie theaters were full of people and in the direct path of the fire. Firemen and police ordered everyone out of the theaters. Movie goers began to flee, rushing to the exits in pandemonium. People at the front were pushed and shoved as panic set in. Many of the people grabbed each other as they ran, picking up those who had fallen in the melee and dragging them out. Some of them were shocked as they got outside and saw the fire advancing. Some had become separated from their companions and were running around, frantically asking if anyone had seen their friend or sister or some other person they knew. As more fire crews arrived, they shouted for people to make way for them. They unrolled their fire hoses and began spraying water on the burning buildings nearby. Other firemen were wielding axes as they broke down doors and shattered windows so the water could reach the flames inside. Then the firemen quickly moved back as the heat became intense. It was a horrific scene.

Jean and Lil were walking down Pleasant Street heading home when the sirens started blaring. They turned around toward the sounds. In the darkened, smoke-filled sky, they could see a fiery glow above the downtown buildings. Curious people started running in the direction of the fire trucks. Crowds gathered in the streets trying to see what the noise and excitement were all about. Jean spotted her friend Angie and her sister Margaret standing outside their house. "What's going on?" Angie asked. "Look at the sky," said Jean. "It must be a huge fire to light up the sky like that." They all walked together down to North Main Street. They turned and looked down South Main Street toward the blazing red sky but really couldn't see anything except people and a few cars and wagons heading toward the glow. The girls huddled together in a store entrance to protect themselves from the bitter cold wind blowing toward them. After a while they began to see flames flickering above the buildings at the end of their line of vision. Before long the flames had moved up the street toward City Hall, one building at a time. The girls were too cold to stay where they were, so they began walking toward the distant fire. As the wind picked up and shifted directions, more buildings caught fire. The police started rushing up and down the street, telling everyone to clear the area because the fire was moving rapidly into the downtown area. Bells were clanging and sirens were blaring as more fire apparatus headed toward the fire from surrounding communities. The girls decided that they had better head home. Angie and Margaret reached home first and Lil and Jean continued on to their tenement. Many of their neighbors were standing outside on the sidewalks and porches sharing bits and pieces of information they heard about the fire. By now, they could see the fierce red glow in the night sky from as far away as the Flint.

All throughout the night, the firemen struggled to keep the hoses from freezing. Firemen from surrounding towns kept arriving to help fight the fire but the winds continued to spread the flames. The fire had been relentless, quickly engulfing the mill complex and spreading to the Granite Block, up South Main Street, continuing up North Main Street as far north as Bedford Street, miraculously sparing City Hall. The strong winds and freezing temperatures made it impossible to even slow its progress. It continued to burn for more than twelve hours. Altogether, thirty six buildings burned to the ground. Among them were the Herald News, L'Independent Newspaper, the Kresge building, the Rialto and Premier Theatres, the Eagle Restaurant, Hotel

Mohican, Fall River Historical Society, Western Union, Citizens and Union Banks, department stores, lawyers' and doctors' offices. Falling walls, live wires and flying debris caused injuries to over two hundred and fifty people, including firemen and policemen. Amazingly, there were no deaths reported. After the fire, "the heart of the city was a woeful spectacle of ghostly walls and leaning chimneys", as reported in the *Fall River Herald News* the next day. It was so destructive that it became known as "the Great Fire of 1928".

HEADLINES OF THE TIMES

THE FALL RIVER HERALD NEWS

1929

BYRD DISCOVERS VAST NEW LANDS IN ANTARTICA

HAMMER IN BARN REVIVES 37 YR OLD BORDEN MURDER MYSTERY

STEVE KORAKALES MARBLES CHAMPION OF CITY

DR. TRUESDALE GIVEN MEDAL FOR RESEARCH

SEARS & ROEBUCK TO OPEN RETAIL STORE HERE

RED - AMBER - GREEN LIGHTING SYSTEM TO REGULATE TRAFFIC

RUSSIAN ARMY INVADES MANCHURIA

LINDBERGH FINDS ANCIENT MAYAN CITY WHILE FLYING OVER YUCATAN

AUTO CRUSHED AS BRIGHTMAN ST. DRAWBRIDGE OPENED; DRIVER RESCUES MOTHER & SISTER

PRES.HOOVER'S PROSPERITY PROGRAM TO SPEND BILLIONS ON PUBLIC UTILITIES CONSTRUCTION

STOCKS AGAIN PLUNGE TO NEW LOWS; ALL MARKETS FEEL EFFECTS OF COLLAPSE

STOCK MARKET DROPS; EARLY GAINS SLASHED BY NOON; BANKERS TRY TO SUPPORT MARKET

STOCK MARKET STRUGGLES FROM RECORD LOSSES

1929

School was out for the summer. Jean had just finished the fourth grade. She and Angie had been in the same class at Notre Dame de Lourdes School. They were hoping they would be in the same class next September when they started fifth grade. Jean asked Momma if she could go downtown with Angie. Momma wasn't feeling well so she was glad the children were busy. Bernie had gotten a job taking care of two children. Nita and Lil had gone to Lafayette Park to watch the boys play baseball. Momma gave Jean a quarter to buy some milk on her way home.

She and Angie walked along Pleasant Street. They had to dodge the trolley car as they crossed the street. The Rag Man was standing on the corner next to his horse-drawn wagon, calling out to buy rags and bottles. They went past a man pushing a cart with a big stone wheel. He stopped when a woman approached him and asked him to sharpen her dressmaker's shears. He turned the grinding wheel by pushing on a peddle with his foot. The wheel began to spin and sparks began to fly as he sharpened the scissors. The girls watched the sparks and listened to the whirring sound of the wheel. It was mesmerizing.

The two friends continued down the street. As they passed the red brick building housing the Flint Fire Station, they peered in and saw pumpers, engines and ladder trucks. Police Station Number 3 was next to the fire station. They stood on the corner waiting for automobiles and horse-drawn wagons to pass. When it was clear, they crossed the street. As they walked along the next block, they could hear the cheering crowd from Bigberry Stadium on Wordell Street. It was Saturday and the soccer team was playing. During that time, there were many star athletes from the Flint – names like Billy Gonsalves and Bert Patenaude. Soccer was very popular but there were also baseball, softball and boxing matches held at the stadium. There were even midget auto races there. The girls weren't interested in the soccer game though, they were headed for the dock where the Fall River Line came in. They went across South Main Street, down the hill and across the railroad tracks. The train had just come in from Boston and many of the passengers got out and walked over to the dock to board the steamship to Newport. The steamer, *The Commonwealth*, was in port. It was a luxurious ship four hundred and fifty feet long. It was a double-ender and could sail in either direction without turning around. It was the largest passenger ship operating on Long Island Sound. It had a large fancy salon and dining room on the upper deck where passengers had a spectacular view of the passing ships and the countryside. It even had its own orchestra and excellent cuisine. According to advertising in the local newspapers, the dining room had a triple dome ceiling with concealed lighting and was connected with a dance floor. It also had oriental rugs and elaborate furnishings. Presidents including Grant, Arthur, Harrison, Cleveland, Theodore Roosevelt, as well as millionaires such as the Vanderbilts, Astors, Belmonts and Rockefellers travelled on the Fall River Line from New York to Fall River and then boarded the Fall River Railroad to complete their trips to Boston.

The girls thought it was a treat just to see it and hear the steam whistle announcing its arrival and departure. Jean and Angie walked around the dock watching the ladies and gentlemen as they walked from the steamship to the railroad station, admiring their fancy clothes and especially the ladies' feather hats. "Hey Angie, there's Bella and her sister Julie over there," Jean called out as she took Angie's hand and led her toward their friends. As they approached each other, Bella said, "Isn't this grand. You can still hear the orchestra playing down here." The young girls chattered away as they walked along the waterfront. As the sound of the orchestra from the steamship faded, they could hear the music from the carousel. They walked inside the rotunda to watch the colorful dobbie horses going up and down as they whirled around. They could smell the popcorn in the huge corn popper. It smelled so good! Julie said she had a nickel so she bought a large bucket of popcorn. They all sat down on the bench, totally enjoying the unexpected treat. A man pumping an organ grinder came around with a monkey on his shoulder. The girls started giggling as the monkey jumped down and started dancing. He hopped over to Bella and tipped his little hat, then he hopped over to Jean and put his tiny hand out while he looked right at her. She laughed and shook his hand, and then he scurried back to the organ grinder. Angie held out some popcorn. The monkey ran back, grabbed the popcorn and ate it. The girls laughed and giggled at his antics as the man and his monkey moved around the rotunda. The four girls finished the popcorn, then resumed their walk around the waterfront.

It was a beautiful summer day. Ducks and swans swam around between the docks. Large and small sailboats sailed around the harbor. Julie said, "I wish I could stay here all day but it's getting late and we have to go." "I'm glad we ran into you both and thanks for the popcorn. It was yummy," said Jean. "I can't wait to tell Momma." Julie and Bella headed up the hill to South Main Street while Angie and Jean lingered a while longer. As they finally headed home, Jean remembered that Momma wanted her to get some milk. She spotted the milkman on his horse-drawn wagon and she called out to him. "Hi Lenny. I need a bottle of milk," she told him. She handed him the nickel Momma had given her. Jean tucked the milk under her arm. It was getting late now so she and Angie hurried home.

On October twenty-fourth, the New York Stock Exchange experienced an event that became known as *Black Thursday*. After a day of wild trading and sell-offs, the stock market crashed. Over the next several days, the market fluctuated wildly, plunging and rallying then plunging again. Billions of dollars were lost, wiping out thousands of investors. This was just the beginning as America and the rest of the industrialized world spiraled downward into *the Great Depression*. The Midwestern states were having a severe drought that lasted several years. The continuing drought turned the Midwest into the *Dust Bowl*. Crops failed year after year. Farmers lost everything, including their farms. Crop prices dropped by sixty percent. The mining and logging industries collapsed. Banks failed one after another. Construction ground to a standstill. Wages dropped to a pittance. Unemployment climbed to twenty-five percent. Tens of thousands of Americans lost their jobs and their homes. Hard times became even harder.

When Momma turned on the radio to listen to the news, it was so depressing that she turned it off. The children were all at school. Momma had been coughing most of the night and she felt exhausted. She was ironing some shirts for Arthur when Memé came upstairs with her arms full. She said that Florida had been sorting through some of the clothes her children had outgrown and Momma could have them for the girls. Momma began looking through them. She was grateful that Florida always gave her clothes. She had little money to go out and buy them. Arthur's pay had been cut at the mill and she knew he was lucky to have a job. Memé asked her how she was feeling. She said, "Rosanna, you're so pale and you're getting thinner every day. What does the doctor say?" The doctor had told Rosanna that she had TB (tuberculosis). She had been getting run down over many months and having severe coughing spells. Occasionally, she had even coughed up small amounts of blood. She didn't tell Memé this. "He gave me some tonic to take but there's not much more he can do." She answered. "How are things for Florida at the cotton mill," she asked, to change the subject. Memé told her that there had been layoffs, but so far, Florida had not gotten any notice. The hours were long and the pay was poor, but better than nothing. Everyone that had work, lived in fear of losing their jobs.

Florida and her husband both worked at the Durfee Mill. Florida worked as a spinner and her husband Roland was a machinist. Many of the cotton mills of Fall River had already shut down or moved down south where they could get cheaper labor, newer buildings and more modern machinery. Memé said that she read in the paper that in some places, unemployment was as high as twenty percent and was expected to go even higher.

When the children came home, Memé went back downstairs with Florida's children. Rosanna's four girls came in and spied the clothes from their aunt. They started looking through them. Bernie pulled out a pretty cotton dress that she liked but it was way too small for her. "Jean, come over here," she said. "I think this will fit you." "Here, let me help you try it on." After trying it on, Jean said she liked it and brought it to her bedroom. Bernie sorted the rest of the clothes by size and each of the girls found something for themselves. Momma was glad to see them happy.

Momma started preparing supper and Bernie offered to help. They had a few potatoes and a small piece of beef. Bernie peeled and cut the potatoes while Momma cut the beef into small pieces. She simmered the meat until it was tender, and then added some chopped up onion and the potatoes. Bernie found a can of tomatoes in the pantry and added that to the pot. When Arthur got home, they had the beef stew for supper with a loaf of French bread.

HEADLINES OF THE TIMES

THE FALL RIVER HERALD NEWS

1930

CONGRESS WAGES FIGHT TO END PROHIBITION

CHICAGO GANGS RUN WILD; 7 PERSONS MURDERED

PRES. TAFT LIES IN STATE IN CAPITOL ROTUNDA

500 ENTRIES FOR CITY MARBLES TOURNAMENT

FALL RIVER SOCCER TEAM WINS EASTERN FINALS OF NATIONAL AMATEUR CUP CHAMPIONSHIP

LINDBERGH SETS CROSS-COUNTRY FLIGHT RECORD OF LESS THAN 15 HOURS

ADM. BYRD BACK FROM ANTARTIC EXPLORATION

BOBBY JONES WINS BRITISH OPEN GOLF TITLE

SIR ARTHUR CANNON DOYLE DIES; CREATOR OF SHERLOCK HOLMES

DROUGHT DESTROYS CROPS IN OHIO, KANSAS, OKLAHOMA, ILLINOIS, MISSOURI

HOOVER CONFERS ON DROUGHT RELIEF PLAN

PHILANTHROPIST DAVID GUGGENHEIM DIES AT 74

SINCLAIR LEWIS WINS NOBEL PRIZE IN LITERATURE

HOOVER AND CONGRESS SPLIT ON RELIEF FOR UNEMPLOYED

1930

Momma had been ill for a couple of years. She had what was commonly called "consumption". She was always coughing and continued to lose weight. Many days she would be weak and listless. She was always careful to cover her mouth with a handkerchief and washed her handkerchiefs separately to protect the children. There was no cure for tuberculosis in those days. There were no antibiotics. Eventually she began spending more time in bed, with Memé and Aunt Florida coming upstairs to help her. It was March and the weather was cold and damp. Jean and her sisters were playing quietly in their room. Memé brought Momma a cup of tea and begged her to drink it. Jean walked over to Momma's bed. "Are you going to be okay Momma?" she asked. Momma smiled weakly as she tried to reassure her. Memé urged her to go play and let Momma rest.

Bernie went into Momma's room to see how she was. Momma looked up at her and tried to smile. She asked Bernie to come over and sit with her. Momma took Bernie's hand in hers. "Bernie," she said, "I am very sick and I don't know how much longer I will last. I know you're only sixteen and it's a lot to ask, but I'm afraid when I'm gone it will be difficult for you and your sisters. Will you promise me that you will do everything you can to keep the four of you together?" Bernie looked at her with tears in her eyes. "Yes Momma, I promise." Then she placed a cool face cloth on her mother's forehead. She sat next to Momma for a couple of hours until Arthur came into the room, and then she went to bed.

When Jean woke up in the middle of the night, Arthur was pacing the floor. Bernie was standing over Momma's bed shaking her and begging her to wake up. Jean went over to the bed. Arthur told her to go downstairs to Memé's and ask her to come upstairs right away. Jean began to feel afraid. She ran downstairs and banged on the door. She waited for what seemed like an eternity, and then banged on the door again. Finally she started yelling for Memé and Aunt Florida. They both came to the door. When they saw Jean crying, they rushed upstairs. Jean followed them. When they went in, Lil and Nita had gotten up and were standing with Bernie around Momma's bed. She looked grey and didn't move. She wasn't coughing any more but there was a handkerchief in her hand with blood on it. Memé gently closed Momma's eyes. Jean would never forget that day. It was St. Patrick's Day. She was ten years old. Momma was buried in Notre Dame Cemetery.

After Momma died, Arthur and the girls moved a few streets over to be closer to his family. Arthur started stopping off at the local bar after work. He would often be drunk by the time he got home, sometimes late in the evening. Bernie would look after her sisters and make supper when Arthur came home late. One morning, Bernie got her sisters up and they all got dressed for school. Then they went into the kitchen to have breakfast. Arthur grabbed his lunch pail and left for work without saying a word to anyone. Bernie tried to hurry everyone along but they all seemed to be stuck in slow motion. "Life must go on," she thought. Jean was sitting at the table motionless, then, she started crying. Bernie asked her what was wrong, but she knew. She looked at Lil and saw tears starting down her face. Nita sat quietly staring into space. It had been six months since Momma died but it hadn't gotten any better. Bernie went over to Jean and put her arms around her. "I miss Momma so much," Jean cried. "I know, Jean. We all do," said Bernie. "I wish she was here. She always made me laugh when I was sad. We used to play paper dolls and we would sing songs. I don't feel like singing anymore," Jean lamented. Lil said she didn't want to go to school. She just wanted to stay home and do nothing. Nita continued to stare into space as if she were lifeless. Bernie started talking about all the little things Momma use to do for them – brushing their hair, fixing their clothes, letting them buy penny candy when they went downtown. Lil said she missed the chocolate cupcakes Momma use to make, and the little French pastries.

Bernie looked at the clock and realized that it was too late to get to school on time, so she asked her sisters if they would like to go to the cemetery to see Momma's grave. Nita suddenly responded by getting her coat. She said, "Let's go." Her sisters grabbed their coats and they all walked to the cemetery together. When they got to the grave where Momma was buried, Bernie said, "Let's each of us tell Momma what we wish we could say to her." Bernie started by saying, "Momma, I hope we can always stay together. I love my sisters so much and without you here, I'm afraid to lose them." Nita said, "Momma,

46

sometimes I think I hear you singing in the kitchen, but when I get there – you're not there and I feel all alone." When it was Lil's turn, she said, "Momma, if you could come back, I would always be good and would never start any trouble." Jean stood before the grave with tears streaming down her cheeks and said, "I hope you and little Robert are looking down at us and watching over us so we won't be so lonely." They stayed for quite a while looking at the little headstone that marked Momma's grave. Jean looked around at the graves nearby and saw one with a large spray of flowers beside it. She walked over to it and gently picked out a few of them and placed them next to Momma's gravestone. She looked at Bernie sheepishly and said, "They won't mind, will they?" Bernie said, "I don't think so," and put her arm around Jean's shoulders. "Let's stop by and see Memé on the way home."

After a while, the sisters started for home. When they reached Memé's house, they knocked on the door. When she opened the door, she asked them why they weren't in school. Bernie said they needed to go see Momma. Memé understood. She told them to come in and gave them some cookies and milk, then, she sat down with them while they ate. When they were done, she asked them if they were going to be okay. They all shook their heads affirmatively. "How is Arthur doing?" she asked Bernie. She answered, "He just sits around and stares at the floor when he's home. Sometimes he goes out walking and sometimes when he comes back, he smells like beer. Then he lies on the couch and falls asleep." Memé shook her head and said, "He misses your Momma too. This is the second time he has been left a widow. He must be very sad." The girls sat with Memé for a while talking about Momma and how hard it was without her. It seemed to help to talk about how they felt. After a while, they were ready to go home. Memé kissed each of them and held them close. When they got home, they each wrote a short note to Momma and placed it under their bed pillows.

It was getting late one evening when the girls were home alone. Arthur had not come home yet. Bernie got everyone ready for bed. Lil had fallen and hurt her ankle at school that day and she was crying. Bernie told her to get in bed and it would stop hurting. After a while the house grew quiet. The girls had settled down and gone to sleep.

When Bernie woke up, the house was dark. She didn't know what time it was. As she rolled over, she heard whimpering coming from the next room. Lil's ankle must be hurting, she thought. She heard some noise coming from the other room but she was too sleepy to care. She turned over and dozed off. More noise came from the other room and Bernie woke up again. This time she sat up and listened. She could hear Lil mumbling. It sounded like, "No, don't do that." Bernie got out of bed and went to the next room. As she opened the door, she saw a large dark form on Lil's bed. She heard Lil say, "No, don't." Bernie ran to the side of the bed and grabbed the figure on the bed, pulling it onto the floor. She smelled beer and heard a deep mumbling sound and realized it was Arthur.

She knew he was drunk. While he was still on the floor, she punched him as hard as she could. He managed to get up and headed for the door. Bernie chased after him while hitting him on his back again and again. Arthur finally made it to the door and ran out stumbling along the way. Bernie sat on the bed and put her arms around her younger sister, reassuring her that he was gone. Lil told Bernie that he was touching her and she was scared.

It was a long night. Bernie lay awake wondering what she should do if Arthur came back. Every little sound startled her. She thought about Momma. She thought, "This would never have happened if Momma was here." Sadness enveloped her like a heavy blanket. She slid further into the bed and began to cry softly. "No," she thought, "I must stay strong so I can look after my sisters like I promised Momma I would. I must stay strong," as she wiped her tears away.

Morning came slowly as the light gradually crept across the wall. Bernie was already thinking about what she must do. Finally she made up her mind. She got her sisters up and dressed. She made them some toast and gave them some milk, and then they all went to see their grandmother. Bernie told Memé what had happened last night. She told her that she was afraid to stay with Arthur when he was drunk. "We don't want to live with him anymore," she said. Memé looked at Aunt Florida. She said, "We can't send them back there. What are we going to do?" Aunt Florida shook her head. "We have a full house already. We can't really take them all in." Florida had five children of her own that Memé helped her care for while she worked. "Bernie is only sixteen. She can't be responsible for all her sisters," she added. Bernie pleaded, "I promised Momma I would keep us together Memé. I have to keep my promise. I have to keep us together."

Bernie and Nita had left school to take jobs doing housework for two Jewish families. Lil and Jean were still in school. It was decided that Bernie and Nita would stay with Florida until they could find live-in housework. Lil and Jean would have to go to the orphanage until Bernie was eighteen. Then she would get a flat and take them in.

———————

Aunt Florida walked with Jean and Lil to the orphanage several blocks away. They each carried a small bag with some clothes. The orphans' home was in a large stone building with four stories taking up most of the city block. It was set back from the street with the lawn in front and a few trees around the building. They approached the entrance and rang the doorbell. A woman opened the door and let them inside. Aunt Florida said," I spoke to Sister Beatrice on the phone. She is expecting us." The woman told them to wait in the foyer for Sister Beatrice. Aunt Florida said to Jean and Lil, "I'm late for work so I need to go. Do what the sisters tell you to do and you'll be fine. Remember, this is only temporary. I'll come with Bernie to see you on Saturday." She gave them each a kiss and left.

Jean and Lil stood in the large foyer of St. Joseph's Orphans Home. It was run by the Grey Nuns of Quebec under the auspices of the Notre Dame Church. There was a staircase coming down on one side of the foyer and a long hall going down the other side. A nun came into the foyer and said to them, "Follow me." The two sisters stayed close to each other as they were led to an office behind the staircase. Jean said to Lil, "where is she taking us?" "Shhh!" Lil responded with her finger to her lips. "Don't make her mad." As they entered the office, Sister Beatrice whirled around to face them. She was a very large woman with a stern face. Her habit flowed out as she walked, as if it was trying to keep up with her. Her dark eyes flared at them. They made Jean think of the black cat that lived next door as it stalked a mouse, ready to pounce at the right moment. Her voice was deep as she rumbled instructions at the girls. "Sit! Tell me how old you are." "I'm twelve and my sister is ten," said Lil, while trying not to tremble. Jean squeezed her hand tightly. Another nun came into the room. She was slender and small compared to Sister Beatrice and much younger. "Sister Anne, take the younger one to the children's wing and this one can go with the older girls," ordered Sister Beatrice. "Please," Jean begged, "I want to stay with my sister. I'll be eleven in June." Sister Anne looked up at Sister Beatrice. "Couldn't we keep them together? They're almost the same age." Sister Beatrice glowered at Jean menacingly. "She's too small. She won't be able to keep up with her work," she said. "I will. I will. I can work hard. You'll see," Jean pleaded. Sister Beatrice turned away. Her sharp features reminded Jean of a scarecrow and sent a shiver through her little body. As she towered over Jean, she said, "You must do the same work as the older girls if you want to be with your sister. I'll be watching. Don't you forget! Show them upstairs Sister Anne and tell them the routine."

Sister Anne led them up the long staircase and down the hall into a large room with six beds – two on each of three of the walls. They were each covered neatly with a thin white bedspread. There was a small wooden bureau between each pair of beds. There was one light on the ceiling. The rest of the room was bare. You can put your things in that bureau. You each have two drawers and these are your beds. Sister Anne pointed to the left side of the room. You'll be sharing this room with four other girls. Their names are Amy, Anna, Celeste and Nichole. You get up at the 5:30 bell, get dressed and ready for breakfast by 6:00. Mass is at 7:00. School starts at 8:00 sharp. After school you will be given chores doing laundry, washing floors, cleaning rooms, or preparing food for dinner. You'll be told what you must do every day. You must finish your chores by dinner time which is at 6:00 P.M. Bedtime is at 8:00. Come with me now and I'll take you to the school building next door. We'll put each of you in the proper class and you'll stay there for the rest of the day.

After a few weeks, Jean and Lil began to get use to the routine - up early, go to Mass. Go to school, do your chores. It was hard to keep up with Lil and the older girls and Jean would often be scolded by Sr. Beatrice for not going fast enough. She would threaten to put her with the younger girls and Jean would push herself harder. She wanted desperately to stay with her sister Lil. She missed Momma and her sisters terribly – especially Bernie who always looked after her. One morning, Jean did not feel well. She had had an earache during the night. She often had earaches. Sometimes there would be drainage coming out and trickling down her neck. Momma used to bathe her ear with warm water so that it wouldn't smell badly, but now that Momma was gone, there was no one to do that for her. Some of the children at the orphanage began to call her "stinky ear" in French and she would hide from them when she could. It was Saturday and after Mass, she had to scrub the floor in the hallway upstairs. She thought that if she kept busy, her ear would not hurt so much. She filled her pail with water and soap and grabbed her scrub brush.

As she scrubbed the floor on her hands and knees, her ear throbbed. Sr. Anne walked by and noticed tears streaming down her cheeks. "What's the matter Jean? Why are you crying?" she asked. "My ear aches and it won't stop," she told her. Sr. Beatrice was walking the hall, inspecting the work. Sr. Anne approached her and told her that Jean had an earache. "When she's done her chores she can lie down on her bed," she said impatiently as she hurried by without stopping. Sr. Anne turned around and started walking with her. Jean could hear her pleading with Sr. Beatrice to let Jean lie down now, to no avail. Sr. Beatrice told her that she was too soft-hearted and the children would take advantage of her whenever they could.

As Jean neared the stairway, her earache intensified. She sat on the top step and bounced her way down the stairs in an attempt to ease the pain. It helped a little. She did it again. St. Beatrice had gone down the back stairs and come around to the bottom of the front stairway. She saw Jean land on the bottom step, get up and start back up the stairs. Sr. Beatrice grabbed Jean by the arm and jerked her around. "This isn't a playground," she bellowed, "You've gotten your clothes all dirty with your little game. Just for that, you can scrub the stairs when you have finished the hallway. I think it's time you worked in the laundry room as well." Jean looked up at Sr. Beatrice who was grasping her by both arms and shaking her to attention. Her dark brown eyes felt like they would bore right through her little body. Jean was petrified as the nun raised her hand to strike her. Jean pulled away falling backward onto the stairs. Sr. Anne appeared at the top of the stairs. Sr. Beatrice looked up at Sr. Anne and diverted her eyes back to Jean, trying to hide the anger in them. She told Jean to get her work done, and then she quickly turned and walked away with her long black habit flowing behind her. All she needs is a witch's broom, thought Jean as she went back up the stairs to finish scrubbing the floor before Sr. Beatrice came back.

———————

Jean and Lil had been at the orphanage for six months. One morning after being sick for two weeks, Lil started coughing up green phlegm. Jean was worried about her. She asked, "Are you alright Lil? Should I tell Sister you are sick?" Lil said no. Her face was pale and drawn but she managed to pull on her clothes and head for the dining hall. She felt very weak. Jean helped her down the stairs. The girls lined up on one side of the dining hall and the boys lined up on the other side. Sr. Ruth told Lil to stand up straight. Lil tried to stand tall but she began to cough in spasms. Jean tried to hold her up as she slumped against the wall. Sr. Ruth put her hands on Lil's face. "This child is burning up. She can hardly stand. Sr. Anne, help me take her to the infirmary," she said. Jean began to follow but Sr. Ruth told her to go back to her place and have her breakfast. Jean finished her breakfast and went to Mass. She prayed to God to make her sister well. All during the school day, Jean thought about Lil. She felt so alone and abandoned.

When school was over, she went to the infirmary. She searched every room and every bed but could not find her sister anywhere. She began to panic. "Where is she?" she asked the nun at the desk. "Who, and what are you doing here?" she demanded. "My sister Lil, she's been sick. They brought her here this morning. Please, where is she?" Jean begged. "Alright, that must be the girl we sent to the hospital," said Sister. "When will she be back?" Jean asked, bewildered. Sister told her that she would probably be in the hospital for several weeks, and that she probably had pneumonia. "Now you had better go back downstairs and get your chores done," Sister told her.

Jean wandered back to her assigned cleaning area. She grabbed a pail and mop and began washing the floor in the girls' lavatory. Several other girls were scurrying around cleaning the sinks and toilets. Jean was the smallest and youngest but Sr. Beatrice did not let up on her, not for a minute. Jean was petrified of Sr. Beatrice and tried to hide behind the older girls whenever she came around. She would always arrive in a huff with her habit streaming behind her like a ghost. She was always angry, scolding and chiding each girl as she passed. Jean thought of her as the devil in a habit.

At the end of the day, Jean went to her room and got into bed. Her roommates asked about Lil and she told them that she had been taken to the hospital. Amy wanted to know if she was going to die. Jean just shook her head. This had not occurred to her but now she began to worry. She tossed and turned for hours. Finally, she woke up in a panic. She was afraid she would never see Lil or her family again. She huddled under her blanket unable to sleep for the rest of the night. When morning finally came, Jean looked at Lil's empty bed. She thought about her mother and her other sisters. She felt incredibly alone.

On Saturday morning, Jean began pacing around the visitors' room. There were only two visitors all day until afternoon. Finally Jean saw Bernie come in and ran to her, tears welling up in her eyes. Bernie gave her a big hug. Jean put her arms around her and would not let go. "Where's Lil," Bernie asked. "She's in the hospital. She has "namonia". Amy says she could die," said Jean and the tears streamed down her face. Bernie took Jean's hand and went looking for Sr. Beatrice. She was nowhere to be found. The more Bernie searched, the more angry she became. When she finally saw a nun, she grabbed her by her habit and demanded to know why no one let the family know about Lil being taken to the hospital. The nun said to her, "This is an orphanage. These children have no family. Now you had better quiet down or you'll have to leave." Bernie whirled around, pulling Jean by the hand and headed for the door. "We have a family," she yelled back and flew out the door with Jean running to keep up. They headed for Flint Street and Memé's house.

A week later, Lil was brought back to the orphanage, still pale and weak but eager to see Jean. Sr. Anne greeted her and took her up to her room. When she asked where Jean was, Sr. Anne told her that her sister Bernie had come and taken her out. She didn't know where they had gone but they didn't come back. Sister told her to lie down on her bed and rest before lunch. Lil lay down on the bed. The room was quiet. The other beds were empty and neatly covered with their thin bedspreads. The only other furniture in the room were the three little bureaus between the beds. The walls were bare. There was an old thin greying curtain hanging over the single window. Lil imagined she was all alone in a deep dark cave. She shivered at the thought, and then closed her eyes. She began to think about her sisters. What if Bernie didn't come back to see her. What if they forgot about her. She opened her eyes in a panic. "Where did Bernie go with Jean," she thought. They must have gone to Memé's. There was no way she was going to stay at the orphanage alone. She quietly made her way down the hall, down the stairs and out the main entrance. She walked as fast as she could but she was still weak from being sick and in the hospital. Flint Street seemed far away. When she finally arrived at Memés' she was exhausted.

Bernie and Jean had been staying with Aunt Florida and Memé while Lil was in the hospital. Nita was fourteen and out of school. She was able to find a live-in housekeeping job in the center of town and only spent weekends with them. With Lil's arrival, it was impossible to provide for all of them and Aunt Florida's five children. Bernie said that she would find a small flat for them, but Memé knew that they would need an adult to stay with them, sense Bernie was only sixteen years old. "Please Memé, will you stay with us?" Bernie pleaded, "I promised Momma that I would keep us all together." "Bernie, it's not that I don't want to, but I live with Florida so that I can take care of her children, because she needs to work," Memé answered. "Maybe we can ask your Aunt Tin," Aunt Florida suggested. "She has no children and since her divorce, she has been living alone. Her flat even has an extra bedroom."

Tin was the youngest of Memé's daughters. Her name was Christina but everyone called her by her nickname. She had always been the renegade and seemed to enjoy shocking people. She frequently caused trouble at school in her younger days. Being the youngest, she thought she could get away with anything, and frequently did. In spite of her naughty behavior, she was able to charm her way out of any punishment. She would charm the boys too. They were always hanging around her and she loved the attention. She married when she was eighteen, but soon discovered that marriage brought responsibilities and expectations. Her husband, Herbert, expected her to settle down after they were married, but she was not ready for that. She was a child of the "Roaring Twenties" and she loved to go out partying. Herbert worked for a company that set up machinery for manufacturers moving to new locations or setting up a new factory. He travelled a great deal for his job, leaving Tin on her own much of the time. When he was home, Tin would want to go out, and he would want to stay home and relax. They would argue and fight frequently. It was no surprise when they decided on a divorce after two years of marriage.

After talking it over, Memé and Bernie walked over to Aunt Tin's flat a few streets over. She was not thrilled to see them. She listened to what they had to say, then quickly came up with reasons why their staying there wouldn't work. "It would be pretty crowded you know." reasoned Tin. Bernie told her that Nita had left school and had a live-in job. She would only be there on her days off. "I have a job doing housework too, so we can help pay the rent," Bernie reasoned. "I can be here when Jean and Lil are home from school and as soon as Lil is a little older, she will be able to work after school too". "Well I don't want to be tied down," said Tin, "I like to go out dancing and be with my friends you know." Bernie said, "You only have to be here when the city worker comes to check on us. I'll look after my sisters and do the cleaning." Tin began to think about the rent money she would be able to save for herself. Finally she told them, "You'll have to share the other bedroom and you'll have to do chores like cooking and cleaning and washing clothes. You're all big enough to take care of yourselves." So it was decided.

Memé and Aunt Florida were able to beg and borrow two beds and a couple of bureaus from relatives so the girls would have a place for their things. Uncle Albert lived across the hall from Tin and he helped them move the furniture in. Jean and Lil would share one bed and Nita could share the other with Bernie on the nights when she would not be working.

Because the girls were orphaned, and underage, the city social worker began making regular visits to them to make sure they were living with a responsible adult. She asked Tin many questions about their living arrangements and Tin assured her that she would make sure they all had what they needed. Tin made many promises but the girls soon learned that they had to fend for themselves. Tin worked as a clerk in the Five-and-Ten-Cent store and in her free time, she would go out partying with her friends. Memé did not approve of her lifestyle and the fact that she was divorced, but Tin was always headstrong and fiercely independent. Memé was very grateful that she let the girls move in with her and knew she needed to tread lightly under the circumstances.

HEADLINES OF THE TIMES

THE FALL RIVER HERALD NEWS

1931

RAILROADS, AUTO PLANTS TAKE ON NEW WORKERS

AID FOR DROUGHT VICTIMS SENT TO HOOVER

MILK FUND DWINDLING WHILE NEED CONTINUES

SEWING INTRODUCED AT DURFEE TEXTILE SCHOOL

WORLD HEARS POPE PIUS XI'S RADIO ADDRESS

IRON WORKS TO REOPEN; MEANS 400 JOBS

PROHIBITION ENTERS 12TH YEAR TODAY

NOTRE DAME COACH KNUTE ROCKNE DIES IN PLANE
CRASH; DEATH A NATIONAL LOSS SAYS HOOVER

AL "SCARFACE" CAPONE PLEADS GUILTY TO TAX
EVASION; BROUGHT DOWN BY FED ELIOT NESS

CAPITAL OF MANCHURIA SEIZED BY JAPANESE;
CHINA APPEALS TO LEAGUE OF NATIONS

FAMOUS YACHTSMAN SIR THOMAS LIPTON DIES

MOURNING WORLD PAYS HOMAGE TO INVENTOR
THOMAS EDISON

JAPAN MARCHES FROM MANCHURIA TO MONGOLIA

RIOTS RAGE IN INDIA AS GANDHI RETURNS

1931

As the youngest of four girls, all of Jean's clothes were hand-me-downs from her sisters. Nothing fit her properly. Most of her dresses were either too long or too short and all of them were well worn and faded by the time they came to her. She often felt like a street urchin. When she was in school, some of the other children made fun of her, even though some of them were not much better off than she. *The Great Depression* made an indelible mark on her generation. Many died at a young age due to poor nutrition, illness and lack of money for doctors and medicines. Many nights were spent at home huddled together, trying to keep warm because there was no money for coal to put in the stove for heat. There was never enough to eat either.

Jean was often left home alone in their flat on Fourteenth Street when her Aunt Tin would go out and Lil and Nita would go dancing. Jean was too young to go with them. When Bernie was seventeen, she met a dashing young man whose name was Aime LaCroix. She spent much of her free time with him and their friends. When Jean was alone, she would often think about Momma. She wondered what it would be like if she were still alive and she would daydream about playing paper dolls with her. She remembered when she would cut out the dolls and clothes from the newspaper that the neighbors saved for Momma. She and Momma would give the paper dolls names and make up stories to play out with them.

The flat that the girls and Aunt Tin lived in had no bathroom. There was a toilet in a tiny room at the end of the hall that was shared by the two families living on the same floor. There was a little sink to wash in. The toilet had a tank on the wall high above and a long chain to flush it. There was no window and it was always dark. Jean was afraid to use it when she was home alone. As she made her way down the dimly lit hall, she would hear voices and noises coming from the other tenements. She often saw shadows on the walls and she would imagine that someone was watching her. When she got to the bathroom, she would open the door, reach into the dark and feel along the wall for the chain to turn on the light. Sometimes her hand would hit the towel bar which never had any towel on it. This would make her jump, fearing that someone was trying to grab her hand. When she finally hurried back to the flat, all kinds of frightening thoughts would be dancing around in her head.

One night when she was home alone, Aunt Tin came in with a man. She told Jean that they were going into her room to talk. They went in and shut the door. Tin liked to go out and party with friends but this was the first time she came home with a man. Jean was sitting in the kitchen when she heard sounds coming from Tin's room. She wondered what they were doing. After a while she heard moaning, softly at first and then louder. She got scared. She thought the man must be beating her Aunt Tim and she began to scream. Uncle Albert, who lived across the hall, heard her screams and came running in. "What's the matter," he asked and Jean pointed to the door of Tin's room. "They're in there," she cried. Albert barged through the door. He saw Tin lying on the bed with a stranger. He grabbed the man and dragged him out of the room, as he scrambled to get his pants up. Albert pushed him out into the hall, cursing him and threatening to beat him up if he ever came back, then, Albert went back into Tin's room. Jean could hear them arguing loudly. He called Tin a tramp and she told him to mind his own business. Albert stormed out of the room and went back to his flat. Jean just sat there, not sure what had happened. When Tin finally came out of her room, she looked at Jean with fury in her eyes. "You little trouble-maker! You had better keep your mouth shut about this," she said. Jean got up and ran into her own room, closed the door and waited for her sisters to come home.

The sun shone brightly although the trees were bare and the temperature never got above freezing. Jean wrapped her coat tightly around her. It was too big for her but it was the only coat she had. It had been her sister Lil's and Nita's before that. It was made of faded blue wool. It was worn around the elbows and the corners of the pockets were torn. The lining hung below the bottom of the coat. Jean hurried along Pleasant Street, past the Five-and-Ten-Cent store, the diner and the furniture store in the Flint neighborhood. As she neared the corner, she saw the trolley car whiz by, creating a rush of air that threatened to knock her over.

She turned the corner and headed for Angie's house. Angie was her best friend. She had known her since first grade. Her mother had died too. She lived with her father and two older sisters. Jean walked up to the house and knocked on the door. She heard footsteps approach and the door opened. "Hi Angie," she said. "Can you come out?" Angie smiled and said," my sister gave me a dime to go to the movies with Cecil. Can you come with us?" If only someone would give her a dime, Jean thought. "No I can't go today Angie," she said. She turned around and headed home. She felt very much alone. No one ever gave her a dime to go to the movies.

Jean put on her worn and faded dress. It was tight around the waist and way too short, despite her small stature. She tried to adjust it by wriggling as she pulled it down. It was no use. She went to her sister Nita and asked her if she had a dress to give her. Nita pulled one of the dresses that Bernie had given her from her drawer. She didn't like it because it was too loose and had two buttons missing on it. She told Jean that she could have it if she spent Saturday helping her at her job doing housework for Mrs. Wiseman.

On Saturday morning, Jean went with Nita to Mrs. Wiseman's home. Nita told her that her younger sister would be helping her with the cleaning. Mrs. Wiseman told her to make sure she did a good job or Nita would have to do it over again. Nita showed Jean where the bucket and scrub brush were and told her to scrub the kitchen floor and the stairs and to make sure she changed the water often. Jean filled the bucket at the sink, grabbed the soap and scrub brush and began scrubbing on her hands and knees. The bucket was heavy and she had difficulty lifting it up to empty it into the sink. After dumping the dirty water out, she filled the bucket with clean water. Each time she lifted the full bucket and carried it back to where she had left off, it seemed to get heavier. By the time she finished the kitchen floor and stairs, she was exhausted. Nita had been ironing and folding clothes and putting them away. She told Jean that she had to wash and dry the dishes before they could go home. When she said she was tired, Nita said, "If you want the dress, you have to do it." When Jean was finally done, she and Nita went home.

Jean opened the door and slowly walked inside. All she could think of was lying down to rest. Bernie looked at her and looked at Nita. "What did you make her do?" she asked. "Oh, she just scrubbed the kitchen floor and stairs and washed some dishes – that's all," Nita answered. "What's wrong with you, Nita. She's only eleven years old and you're fifteen. What did you make her do all that for?" Bernie demanded. Nita told her that Jean wanted one of her dresses so she had to help her at Mrs. Wiseman's. "I don't know why you're so mean to her," scolded Bernie. "Momma would never let you do that," she added as she stormed out of the room.

The next day, Jean put on the dress that Nita had given her. It was much too big for her but at least it was not too tight or too short. Actually, it hung down almost to her ankles. This was Sunday and she wanted to go see her friend Angie. Aunt Tin was still sleeping. She had been out late last night. Jean knew better than to disturb her. Bernie was in the kitchen looking for something to eat. She found some bread and bananas and shared them with her sisters. After they all went to Mass, Jean told Bernie that she was going over to Angie's. It was a cool morning so Jean put her sweater on. The sun was shining and she felt good to be out. It was pretty quiet, being a Sunday morning. The stores were all closed and there weren't many people out yet. When she got to Angie's and knocked on the door, Angie's father answered. He invited her in and called Angie. The house was small but there was a nice sofa, two upholstered chairs and a big radio in the parlor and a carpet on the floor. Jean had never lived in such a nice place. Angie and her two older sisters were sitting in the parlor talking and listening to the radio. Angie's oldest sister Margaret told Jean to come in and sit with them.

They talked for a while and then Angie asked Jean if she had on a new dress. She said yes, then felt embarrassed that it was too big for her. She told her that Nita had given it to her. Margaret smiled then said, "It's a little long. I could shorten it for you if you would like me to." "You would do that for me?" Jean asked. Margaret said, "Why don't you bring it over tomorrow and leave it with me. I can have it done in a few days." Jean felt grateful and embarrassed at the same time. She wasn't used to having anyone do something nice for her even though she had three older sisters.　She envied her friend Angie even though she didn't have a mother either.

HEADLINES OF THE TIMES

THE FALL RIVER HERALD NEWS

1932

LINDBERGH BABY KIDNAPPED FROM CRIB

U.S. SENDS 4 DESTROYERS TO SINO-JAPANESE CONFLICT

GANDHI MADE PRISONER IN INDIA'S CAMPAIGN FOR INDEPENDENCE

HITLER LIKELY TO HEAD GERMAN CABINET

THREE CENTS POSTAGE RATE EFFECTIVE JULY 6TH

MAJOR JAMES DOOLITTLE EXCEEDS 293 MI/HR RECORD IN PLANE

LINDBERGH BABY MURDERED; BODY FOUND 5 MILES FROM HOME

TANKER WRECKS SLADE'S FERRY BRIDGE

AMELIA FLIES NONSTOP ACROSS U.S. IN 19 HRS

PREMIER OF JAPAN ASSASSINATED

ROOSEVELT SWEEPS NATION; TREMENDOUS VICTORY FOR DEMOCRATS

BANDITS STEAL ARKRIGHT MILL PAYROLL OF OVER 1100 EMPLOYEES

1932

It was early October and the weather was turning cold. The trees were dropping their red, orange and gold leaves in greater numbers each day. Winter was quickly approaching. Jean carefully cut pieces of cardboard to fit inside her shoes in order to cover the holes in the soles. There was no money to buy new ones. When Aunt Tin saw what she was doing, she told Jean to go to Notre Dame Church and tell the priest she needed new shoes for walking to school. Jean put on her coat and headed for the church. It was a long walk and she was very tired when she got there. She went inside the church. There was no one there. She sat down to rest and began to think about Momma. If she were still alive, things would be different – better she thought. If only...... As she thought, she gazed around the church. She had been coming here for as long as she could remember. Most of the French people who lived up the Flint belonged to Notre Dame Church. The priests and nuns all spoke French. The nuns ran the Notre Dame School and taught some of the subjects in French. This gave the parishioners a sense of security and belonging, as most of them or their parents were French-Canadians from Quebec and had come to Fall River in search of work in the textile mills.

The church was very beautiful with its twin copper spires. Inside there were ornate sculptured angels, stone columns and arches. On the ceiling was a painting of, *The Last Judgement,* by the renowned artist, Master Ludovico Cremonini. It made Jean wonder what heaven was like.

She also wondered if Momma was looking down on her from there. It gave her comfort to think so.

One of the nuns came out of the vestry and walked toward the altar. She did not seem to notice Jean sitting in the pew as she placed a long lace scarf across the altar. Jean watched her as she seemed to float along in her habit, slowly crossing in front of the altar, genuflecting gracefully as she passed the tabernacle and continuing to the other side. Jean began to cough and the nun turned toward the sound. When she saw Jean, she walked over to where she was seated. "May I help you?" she asked, as she looked at Jean's thread-bare coat and worn out shoes. Jean looked at her with an embarrassed smile. The nun smiled back and asked if she needed anything. Jean felt encouraged and told her that the soles of her shoes had worn through and she needed new ones to walk to school in. "Come with me," said the nun and she led her to the rectory. Then she asked her name. "Did someone send you here?" she asked. "Yes," Jean answered, "my aunt told me to come and ask the priest for new shoes." "Do you live with your aunt?" the nun asked. "Yes, I've lived with her and my three sisters since Momma died," Jean explained. "And your father?" she asked gently. "He died when I was a baby," Jean answered. She didn't mention her stepfather.

"I'll take you to Father John," she said and led her down the hall and into his office. "Father John, this is Jean Berthiaume. She is living with her aunt and sisters since her mother and father have both died. She is in need of new shoes. Can you help her?" asked the nun. Father John was sitting at his desk. He slowly raised his eyes and looked at Jean. He looked very old to Jean. He was heavy set and somewhat gruff as he spoke. "You need shoes do you? Let me see the ones you are wearing," he said. Jean sat down on the chair near the door and raised her feet so that he could see the soles of her shoes. He got up and reached for his coat. He told the nun that he would take Jean to the store for shoes. "Come child, follow me," he said and Jean followed behind him.

Jean had to walk quickly to keep up with Father John. He never looked back to see if she was there and she was afraid she would lose him. When they got to the shoe store, he opened the door and motioned for Jean to go in ahead of him. "This child needs a pair of shoes," he said to the clerk. They must be sturdy but not expensive." The clerk measured Jean's foot, then went into the backroom. When he came back, he had two pairs of shoes. He put the first pair on Jean's feet and had her walk in them. They were dark brown and rather plain but Jean thought they were pretty. Then he put the second pair on her feet. They were black and bulky looking, like work boots. "Which pair costs less?" asked Father John. "These," said the clerk, pointing to the shoes Jean still had on. The priest said those were the ones he wanted. Jean looked at the first pair. They were so much prettier, she thought, but she didn't dare say anything.

Father John led her out of the store wearing the black shoes. He told her to go straight home and to take good care of the shoes because they needed to last her a long time. Then he said he wanted to see her in church every Sunday. "Yes Father," Jean promised and she slowly walked home wishing she had gotten the pretty brown shoes instead of these ugly black ones, but she had learned that beggars can't be choosers.

As Bernie's eighteenth birthday approached, she and Memé started canvassing the neighborhood for a new apartment for the four sisters. After her birthday, she would be old enough to be the guardian for her sisters, and they would no longer need Aunt Tin to keep the city social worker at bay. They finally found a flat on Flint Street just two blocks from where they used to live when Momma was alive, and where Memé and Aunt Florida still lived. They could move in any time after Bernie's birthday.

Bernie had gotten a job as a spinner at the Kerr Thread mill making twelve dollars a week. Nita and Lil had left school after completing eighth grade (as most of their friends did, since the child labor law required them to be at least fourteen to work). They were both doing housework. Jean had a babysitting job after school and on weekends. When they pooled all their money, they had just enough to pay the rent, buy food and have a few dollars for other necessities. Bernie and Jean walked over to the welfare office on Alder Street once a week to get free cans of grapefruit, beans, raisins and prunes. They also were given a check to buy fish at the fish market. On Saturday afternoons, they would go to the market to get fruits and vegetables. That was the time when the shop keepers would lower the prices on the produce, because they would be closed on Sundays and the fruits and vegetables would spoil by Monday. Bernie knew how to get the most for the small amount of money the girls had to live on.

As they walked along Pleasant Street, they saw policeman Jim Merrill walking his beat. He and his fellow policemen were well known to the residents of the Flint. They were always stopping to talk to the residents and shopkeepers. They all knew each other by name and often told the police about any vagrants who were hanging around, or any mischief the local youngsters may have been into. Sometimes they just talked about the local news around town or about sports. Soccer was very popular and there were games going on every weekend at Bigberry Stadium.

Bernie and Jean stopped to talk to policeman Jim. Jim asked how they were doing. Bernie told him that after her birthday next week, she and her sisters would be moving to their own flat on Flint Street. Jim smiled and tipped his hat to Bernie. He knew that she had been looking after her sisters since their mother had died. He had seen her stand up for them and protect them many times and admired her for it. He wished them well and continued on his beat. When they got home, Nita and Lil were home from work and they made plans for Bernie's birthday.

On the big day, they all went to see Memé. Jean, Lil and Nita put up some paper decorations they had made. Aunt Florida brought out her linen tablecloth, which she had gotten as a wedding gift, and placed it on the table.

Memé had given the girls a few dollars to buy a cake and some ice cream. They put them in the middle of the table. Bernie was smiling from ear to ear. This was her first birthday cake since Momma had died. She was very proud that she had been able to keep her promise to Momma. She had kept her sisters together and tomorrow they would move into their own apartment.

HEADLINES OF THE TIMES

THE FALL RIVER HERALD NEWS

1933

FORMER PRESIDENT CALVIN COOLIDGE DIES

ROOSEVELT'S NEW DEAL BEGINS TO TAKE SHAPE

GERMANY SHARPLY DIVIDED AS HITLER BECOMES CHANCELLOR

GERMANY LEAVES LEAGUE OF NATIONS

5 SHOT AS BULLETS MISS PRES-ELECT ROOSEVELT

RUN ON BANKS CAUSE BANKS TO CLOSE FOR 10 DAYS ACROSS NATION

PRESIDENT ROOSEVELT TO SEEK WAR-TIME POWERS TO MEET EMERGENCIES

PRESIDENT UNVEILS PLAN TO CREATE 250,000 JOBS UNDER EMPLOYMENT RELIEF BILL

JAPAN WITHDRAWS FROM LEAGUE OF NATIONS

BEER BILL SIGNED; STATE LIQUOR CONTROL COMMISSSION APPOINTED

FALL RIVER TEXTILE SITUATION MUCH IMPROVED

1600 LOCAL MEN GIVEN WORK IN CIVILIAN WORKS PROJECT; TO BE PAID $15 A WEEK

1933

The Berthiaume girls were living on their own now. They no longer had to worry about the city social worker coming in. They all pitched in with chores and soon settled into a routine. Bernie had a job working in one of the textile mills. Lil and Nita had their housekeeping jobs, and Jean was finishing the eighth grade.

One Saturday morning, Bernie told Jean that she could go over to Angie's house after she finished her chores. When she arrived at Angie's, she was greeted by her older sister Margaret. "Oh Jean," she said, "We were just leaving for a walk downtown. Why don't you come along." "Sure," said Jean. She always enjoyed going downtown to look in the store windows and pretend she had money to buy something. When they reached South Main Street, they passed a shoe store and a dress shop. Margaret stopped to window-shop. She was admiring a lovely emerald colored dress with a lacey bodice and graceful flared skirt. She said to Angie, "Look at that dress. Isn't it just beautiful?" Angie said that she really liked the color and Jean imagined herself going to church all dressed up in it. "Wouldn't that look nice on me," she thought, pretending she could actually afford to buy it. At least it was fun to pretend. The three girls walked by several blocks of stores, peering into the windows and admiring the things they saw.

At last they headed for home. As they walked along, Jean began to look pale as she was having a difficult time catching her breath. "What's wrong?" Margaret asked. Jean said her chest hurt. They were near Angie's house and Margaret told Jean to come in with them. She looked concerned for Jean. When they got inside, she told Jean to sit down and patted her gently on the back. As she did, she felt a band across her back. "Is this your brazier?" she asked, "It seems very tight." Jean said "yes" and was clearly embarrassed. "Why is it so tight?" asked Margaret. "No wonder you are having trouble breathing." Jean looked at her sheepishly and said, "How else can I keep myself flat?" "Oh Jean, a brazier is not to keep you flat, it's to support your breasts." "Didn't your sisters explain about how your body changes as you grow into a woman?" asked Margaret. "No," answered Jean. Angie asked, "Have you started your monthly yet? They must have told you about that." "Not yet, but I've seen bloody rags soaking in a bucket in the bathroom and I heard some girls whispering about it at school," Jean said as she blushed. "Gosh," Margaret responded, "why don't we go to the Women's Clinic on Rock Street? There's a lady doctor there that can explain all of this to you. You really should know these things." "But I have no money to see a doctor," replied Jean. Margaret assured her that the clinic was started by the Women's Union and they didn't charge anything if you had no money. Jean agreed to go if Margaret and Angie would go with her.

The three girls walked to the clinic. It was in-between a clothing store and a drugstore in a three-story wooden building. There was a large store window in the front with a sign in it that said, "Women's Health Clinic". Below it said, "Supported by the Women's Union. All are welcome." Through the window, Jean could see the waiting room which had several benches along the painted walls. There was a large desk near the door and a woman writing at the desk. Margaret signed them in and they were told to take a seat. There were several women ahead of them. As they waited, Jean wondered what these women were there for. One woman kept coughing into her handkerchief. She made Jean think of her mother and how she was always coughing before she died. Another woman was pressing on her stomach as if she was in pain.

Finally it was Jean's turn. She turned to Margaret and Angie. She felt anxious and asked them to come in with her. The three went in together. The lady doctor asked who was the patient, and Margaret pointed to Jean. Jean blushed again. She didn't know what to say. Margaret explained that Jean's mother had died and she needed someone to explain to her about female things. She told the doctor that Jean had been wearing a brazier so tight that she had trouble breathing.

"I'm Doctor Lussier," the doctor began as she placed her hand on Jean's shoulder, patting it lightly. "How old are you Jean?" "I'm fourteen," Jean told her nervously. "Tell me, have you started your monthly period yet?" Jean shook her head "no". "I'm going to tell you what happens when a girl your age grows into a women, and what you need to know about it." She sat down beside her and went on to explain these things to Jean in a gentle reassuring voice, and then she asked if she had any questions. She looked at Jean then Angie and Margaret. They each said no. Margaret thanked the doctor and said, "I tried to explain these things to Angie when she turned twelve but I didn't feel right about explaining it all to Jean, because she's not my sister." "You're a good friend," said the doctor as she led them to the waiting room. "If you have any more questions you can come here any time."

When they left the clinic it was getting late. Margaret and Angie walked Jean home then headed for their house a few blocks away.

HEADLINES OF THE TIMES

THE FALL RIVER HERALD NEWS

1935

PRES. URGES VAST PUBLIC WORKS FOR JOBLESS

HAUPTMANN GETS DEATH SENTENCE FOR KILLING LINDBERGH BABY

SUPREME COURT JUSTICE OLIVER WENDELL HOLMES GIVEN HERO'S BURIAL

URGED NO DELAY TO SOCIAL SECURITY PROGRAM

HITLER WANTS PARITY WITH ARMIES OF EUROPE

MAYOR MURPHY BUYS GIRL SCOUT COOKIES

ENGLAND RUSHES PLANS FOR AIR DEFENSE

FALL RIVER DISTRICT HEADQUARTERS AS WPA PROGRAM GETS UNDERWAY AUGUST 1ST

TWISTER SWEEPS WESTPORT WITH MAJOR DAMAGE

NAZI MOBS LED BY STORM TROOPERS RENEW ATTACKS ON JEWS

BOARD OF HEALTH CLOSES SCHOOLS DUE TO INFANTILE PARALYSIS EPEDEMIC

1935

At the age of fourteen, Jean was old enough to work, so she left school after she finished the eighth grade. During the Depression, many children were forced to leave school at an early age to help support their families. For the next two years, Jean had been doing housework for Mrs. Sol Abraham. It was a live-in job with one day off every Saturday. Mrs. Abraham had a two-and-a-half year old boy that Jean was expected to watch whenever Mrs. Abraham went out to her social meetings and to temple. She was very active in her Jewish community. Jean also watched him when the Abrahams went out in the evenings. Mrs. Abraham loved to cook and she would teach Jean as she helped prepare meals. She also taught her how to bake, as she frequently made cakes and pastries for bake sales held by the Sisterhood of Temple Beth El and for special occasions. Jean liked working for Mrs. Abraham but wished she had more free time to spend with her sisters. She only went home on Friday and Saturday nights if she wasn't needed for baby-sitting.

Lil was working at a Lunch Counter on Pleasant Street. It was a small restaurant but very busy as it was located near many stores and cotton mills. One of the other waitresses had just quit and Lil's boss, Mr. Gagnon, needed to replace her. He asked all the waitresses if they knew anyone who was looking for work. When Lil saw Jean on Friday night, she told her about the job. "The job is eight hours a day Monday through Friday and half-day on Saturday mornings and it pays six dollars a week," she said. "What do you think? You could be home every day after work and you wouldn't have to baby-sit at night." Jean thought about it for a few days. Mrs. Abraham had been very good to her but she really wanted more free time. The pay was better too. She decided to apply for the job. The next day, she asked Mrs. Abraham for some time off to go downtown. Mrs. Abraham let her go in the afternoon.

Jean walked to the restaurant and went inside. Lil was at the lunch counter serving a customer. When she saw Jean, she went over and told her that she had talked to Mr. Gagnon about her. She told Jean to go around to the back office where he would be. Jean walked around to the office and knock on the door. A booming voice told her to come in. Mr. Gagnon was a large burley man. He looked to be about fifty with thinning hair. He had a no-nonsense manner of speaking but a pleasant smile. His trousers were loose fitting and kept up with suspenders. He wore a white shirt with his sleeves rolled up and an open collar.

"I'm Jean Berthiaume, Lil's sister," Jean began. "She said you were looking for a waitress for the lunch counter." Mr. Gagnon looked her over then asked what grade she was in. "Oh, I graduated from eighth grade two years ago," Jean told him. "I won't be going back to school." "What kind of work have you done?" he asked. Jean told him that she had been doing housework since she was fourteen and is sixteen now. She told him she was working for Mrs. Sol Abraham. "Aha, I know Mrs. Abraham. How do you like working for her?" Mr. Gagnon asked. "It's a live-in job. I like her very much but have to work long hours. I do housework during the day and watch her little boy, and then she has me babysit some evenings so that I only get to go home on Friday and Saturday nights." Jean explained. "Are you good at making change?" he asked. She said she was, and told him that she did very well in arithmetic in school. Mr. Gagnon smiled and told her that he would give her a try and if she did well, he would offer her a steady job after a couple of weeks. Then he asked her when she could start. She said that she would like to give Mrs. Abraham a week's notice. He agreed and told her to come back a week from Monday at seven o'clock in the morning. Jean thanked him and headed back to Mrs. Abraham's house.

Things went along smoothly the first two weeks at Jean's new job. Lil showed Jean the routine, how to work the cash register and how to clean and stock the lunch counter. When Mr. Gagnon passed out the paychecks, he told Jean that he was satisfied with her work and he would keep her on. After a few more weeks of working at the lunch counter, Jean felt confident that she knew her job. Lil was still telling her what to do, so Jean told her that she didn't need to do that anymore. Lil continued to order her around, however, and Jean began to resent it. Mr. Gagnon began to take notice and he finally took Lil aside. He told her that Jean did not need any guidance from her any longer and he didn't want her giving Jean directions. She finally backed off and Jean took a sigh of relief.

HEADLINES OF THE TIMES

THE FALL RIVER HERALD NEWS

1937

FRENCH VIEW GERMAN ARMY IN AFRICA AS THREAT

PRES. ROOSEVELT TAKES OATH OF OFFICE 2ND TIME

HUDREDS MISSING IN FLOODS IN MIDWESTERN AND SOUTHERN STATES; 83 KNOWN DEAD

GM CALLS 100,000 BACK TO WORK AT HIGHER PAY

NAZI HORRORS SHOCK EUROPE

DERIGIBLE HINDENGURG EXPLODES & BURNS

GEORGE VI CROWNED IN WESTMINSTER ABBEY

SUPREME COURT UPHOLDS SOCIAL SECURITY ACT

JOHN D. ROCKERFELLER DIES; LEAVES FORTUNE TO JOHN JR AND PHILANTHROPIC ENDEAVORS

STARLET JEAN HARLOW BURIED IN SIMPLE RITES

AMELIA EARHART'S PLANE LOST IN SOUTH PACIFIC; NAVY GIVES UP SEARCH AFTER 16 DAYS

GEHRIG & DIMAGGIO CONNECT IN ALL STAR GAME

COMING OF FIRESTONE COMPANY WAS FALL RIVER NEWS HIGH LIGHT IN 1937

YEAR SAW MANY NEW INDUSTRIES LOCATE IN CITY

1937

Bernie had been dating Aime for seven years. Aime was tall, blonde and debonair. He attracted many friends and was well liked. Bernie was much like him, very sociable and fun to be with. Everyone said they made a great couple. They talked about getting married many times, but Aime wanted to wait until he had a steady job. He was a carpenter and because of the depression, jobs were scarce. When he did find work, it didn't last. Few people were building houses and most businesses were just hanging on. By 1937, the economy was improving very slowly in fits and starts. Firestone Rubber and Tire Company moved into Fall River with 2,000 jobs, and then United Workers and Manufacturers, and Berkshire Spinning Company opened up with more jobs. The future began looking hopeful. In the spring, Aime was offered a construction job in Bridgeport, Connecticut. At last he felt confident that he could afford to get married and start a family, if Bernie would be willing to move to Bridgeport. He proposed and Bernie accepted. There was no time to waste. Aime had to be in Bridgeport in two weeks.

They arranged to be married in a simple ceremony in the rectory of Notre Dame Church. Aunt Florida lent Bernie her wedding dress. Nita and Aime's brother Richard stood up for them. Jean and Lil helped Memé and Aunt Florida prepare a small reception for them at home. Jean used her baking and cooking skills that she had learned from working for Mrs. Abraham, to bake a wedding cake. Bernie's girlfriend, Ida, worked in a bakery and helped Jean frost and decorate it. It turned out to be beautiful and Jean was very proud when Bernie and Aime made the first cut. One of their friends had a camera and took pictures. After everyone ate, Memé took out the Victrola and played some records. The guests rolled up the carpet and they all danced. It was a wonderful celebration.

Two days later, Bernie and Aime packed their things, what little they had, for the move to Bridgeport. Uncle Alcide gave them a ride to the train station. Jean bid them good-bye with feelings of happiness and excitement for them, but sadness for herself. She knew she would miss Bernie a great deal. She had done so much for her three sisters, keeping them together, looking out for them, and protecting them as much as she could. Because Jean was the youngest, she looked up to Bernie the most. She would always have a special place in her heart for her big sister.

———————

When Jean was eighteen, she, Lil and Nita were sharing an apartment. Jean had been working at the restaurant for a little over a year and a half. After working at the lunch counter on a very busy Friday, Jean was headed home. As she passed her neighbor's house, she saw Mrs. LaPierre and her daughter Josephine sitting on their porch. They greeted each other cordially. Jean asked Josephine if she was still living in New Hampshire and working in the sewing shop there. Josephine told her that she was. "I was just telling Momma that the textile mills and garment factories in Exeter are hiring, and offering on-the-job training for new workers." Jean told her that there were jobs in the Fall River Mills and sewing shops but they only wanted experienced workers. Josephine said, "Why don't you come up to Exeter and take the training? Then you could come back to Fall River, join the Ladies' Garment Workers Union, get hired here, and be making good money." "I don't know," replied Jean, "Where would I live? Besides, my family is here." "Maybe your sisters would want to go too," said Josephine. "There are boarding houses in Exeter and the mill owners built tenement houses for the workers with reasonable rents. You could get a tenement for all three of you." Jean said she'd think about it and see what her sisters thought of the idea.

Jean continued on to the flat she shared with Lil and Nita. As she prepared dinner, she thought about going to New Hampshire. It sounded like a good opportunity but the thought of leaving Fall River seemed a bit scary. Still, if she could get a higher paying job, it might be worth it. Lil and Nita came home and the three sisters sat down to dinner. Jean told them about her conversation with Josephine. Together, they discussed the advantages and disadvantages of going to New Hampshire. Lil said if she could make more money working in the mill, she and her boyfriend Joe could get married. Nita said she was tired of doing housework and would like the chance to do something else. So it was decided that they would go to Exeter. Jean agreed to ask Josephine for more details about the job training and the boarding house where they could stay until they could find an apartment. They would share expenses as they were doing in Fall River.

The more they talked about it, the more excited they became. They told Memé and Aunt Florida all about their plans. Florida agreed to keep the few pieces of furniture they owned for them while they were gone. They gave their bosses two weeks' notice and began to pack the clothes and belongings they would take with them. Josephine had already gone back to Exeter and would check on the boarding house for them.

Jean told her friend Angie that she was going to Exeter, New Hampshire with Lil and Nita. "How long will you be gone?" she asked. "I don't know, but I'll write to you," Jean assured her. "I'm going to miss you Angie. You are my best friend." "I'm going to miss you too," Angie replied.

There was so much to do before Jean, Lil and Nita left for New Hampshire, that they were all very busy. They packed, moved furniture and other belongings to Aunt Florida's house, bought tickets for the bus trip, and told all their friends and relatives about their plans. Lil told Joe that she would write to him and Nita promised to write to Stanley, her latest boyfriend. They expected to stay in Exeter for three or four months.

The three sisters left for Exeter on Saturday. The bus trip was long and monotonous. They had to change buses twice before arriving in Exeter. When they finally did arrive, they were tired and hungry. The bus station had a lunch counter where they purchased sandwiches and coffee. Jean felt much better after having something to eat. Lil hailed a taxi outside of the bus station, and the three sisters headed for the boarding house. Josephine had inquired about a room for them so the manager was expecting them when they arrived. They introduced themselves and asked about the room. The manager was Mrs. Elizabeth Plouffe. She was a plump middle-aged woman with a warm smile and cordial manner. She showed them a large room with three beds, a sitting area and two large windows through which the bright sunlight was streaming in. "We rent by the week. We serve meals in the dining room downstairs – family style. Breakfast starts at 6:00 AM, lunch on the weekends at noon and dinner at 6:00 PM. Boarders usually buy their lunch during the week where they work. Most everyone here works at one of the textile mills or sewing shops. They're all young people like you, six ladies and two gentlemen. "

Jean, Nita and Lil began to unpack their bags and settle in. There was a knock on the door. Lil opened the door. It was Josephine. She was glad to see them. She offered to show them around town and invited them to join her for dinner. Josephine told them that she was sharing an apartment with three other girls. Josephine and Rebecca were working in the sewing shop and Suzanne and Catherine were working in the textile mill. They were sharing a third floor tenement with two bedrooms, a small bath, a large kitchen and a small parlor with a door opening onto a porch. There were many similar tenement houses all along the street. Josephine told them that most of the people living in them were young people and families who had moved there from Canada. Jean was eager to meet them since her family had come from Quebec. Maybe she would find someone who knew them.

As they strolled through the town with Josephine, Jean heard several passersby speaking French. They could see several of the mills surrounding the village. It seemed a lot like Fall River. There was a Catholic church at the center of the village and a park across the street from it. People were sitting on the park benches while a group of boys played baseball, and several girls stood by chatting and watching the game.

As they walked to the tenement where Josephine lived, Jean noticed that most of the triple-decker houses along the way had porches on each floor. There were people sitting on many of the porches talking to their neighbors. Josephine said that after they got jobs, she would help them find an apartment. She knew a lot of the women in the neighborhood because they all worked in the mills and they were very friendly. Josephine led them to her tenement. They went up two flights of stairs to the third floor. When they entered the apartment, Rebecca and Catherine were preparing dinner. They told Josephine that Suzanne would be back in a little while. Josephine introduced everyone. They all went into the sitting room and began to talk. Rebecca and Catherine spoke French. Nita asked what part of Canada they came from. They said they were both from Quebec City and Suzanne was from Montreal but had lived in Quebec City for a time. Lil told them that they were from Fall River, Massachusetts but their parents and grandmother had come from Quebec, as well as their aunts and uncles. When Suzanne came in, Josephine introduced her around, then Rebecca and Catherine went back to preparing dinner. In a little while, they all sat down at the dinner table in the kitchen. Lil, Nita and Jean were eager to hear about the jobs that were in the mills and sewing shops and asked many questions. Nita and Lil thought they would like to work in the textile mill, but Jean was interested in learning how to sew in one of the garment manufacturers' sewing shops. Josephine said she would show them the main hiring office and union hall so they would know where to go on Monday to apply for jobs.

On Sunday morning, Lil, Jean and Nita got up early so they could meet Josephine and go to church together. The Mass was celebrated in French just like it was at Notre Dame Church in Fall River. After Mass, they strolled through the park as they talked. They noticed that many of the signs around the village were in both French and English. It was like being back in the Flint. They spent the rest of the day with Josephine and their new friends.

On Monday morning, the three sisters went down to the dining room for breakfast. One of the young men and three of the young ladies were there. They all sat down and introduced themselves. Lucien Bonin was tall, lean and muscular. He was also very friendly. Maria was heavy set, short, with a big smile and mischievous eyes. She made Jean think of her sister Bernie. Mary was just the opposite – thin, petite and rather somber looking. Doris, on the other hand, was very attractive and very talkative. They all switched back and forth between speaking English and French as if it were all one language. Mrs. Plouffe brought out some pancakes and Canadian bacon, toast, jam, orange juice, and coffee for her boarders. It was a very pleasant breakfast.

When everyone was done eating they hurried off to work. Jean, Lil and Nita went to the union hall and hiring office. They got the information they needed and were directed to the buildings where the job openings were that they were interested in. Nita and Lil headed for the Wanskuck Textile Mill office and Jean went to the Hebert Manufacturing Mill where Josephine and Rebecca worked. These two mills were just like many of the other mills surrounding the village. They were built out of stone and brick, three to five stories high with long windows all around the building just a few feet apart for maximum light inside. They all had bell towers built on one side. The bell towers contained the stair wells and they all had a large bell at the top which was rung at the beginning and end of the work day. The work day usually started at 7:00 AM with a one hour break for lunch from noon to 1:00 then ended at 4:00 PM Monday through Friday. Some of the mill workers also worked on Saturday mornings.

Jean entered the office of Hebert Manufacturing, where she told the clerk she wanted to apply for a job sewing. The clerk asked how old she was and whether she had any experience. She told him she was eighteen, and she had no experience but was told she could get on-the-job training. The clerk explained that she could start as an apprentice at a lower salary of $12.75 a week for the first month, then if she did well she would move up to a regular salary which started at $19.75 a week for a forty hour week. Jean was very pleased with that since she never made anywhere near that amount doing housework or working at the lunch counter. The clerk gave her an application and showed her a table where she could sit to fill out the forms. After she completed the application, the clerk explained to her that this was a closed shop and she would have to join the Textile Workers Union to work there. She would also have to pay union dues which could be deducted right from her pay check if she wanted that. Jean knew that all the mills in Fall River were also unionized, so she wasn't surprised.

The clerk took her to the office of the mill foreman who looked over her application and asked her a few questions, and then he asked if she could start right away. Jean's heart was racing with excitement as she said she could. He took her to one of the sewing rooms which was a huge open floor supported by long rows of columns. There were rows of sewing machines from one end to the other. They were being operated by women who worked nearly non-stop making men's clothing. The factory floor was well lit and covered with scraps of cloth, pieces of thread and oil spots. The machines were very noisy and it was difficult for the workers to hear each other speak. They would have to shout to be heard.

The foreman introduced her to the floor supervisor as an inexperienced new-hire. The supervisor's name was Anita L'Etoile. She was around forty-five years old, dark curly hair, dark complexion with a stern expression. She told Jean that as long as she worked hard and minded her own business, they would get along fine. She took her on a quick tour of the work floor, pointing out the ladies' room and explaining the layout of the machines which were grouped according to the type of garments being sewn. Each group was made up of about twenty-five machines and was assigned to a group leader who supervised the workers in her group. All of this was new to Jean and a little overwhelming, but Anita assured her that in a few weeks she would feel right at home. She led Jean to a vacant sewing machine where she would be assigned to work, and then she led her to a small room with a long table and chairs around it. Anita said that she wanted to get away from the noise so that they could hear each other better. She answered Jean's numerous questions, then encouraged her to ask whenever she wasn't sure of anything. She told Jean to be sure she turned in her union papers and told her she was the union steward.

Next, Jean was brought to her work station and introduced to her group leader, Irene Dupont. Irene instructed her on operating the sewing machine and the basics of sewing men's pants. By the end of the day, Jean was tired but happy that she seemed to be catching on pretty quickly to operating the sewing machine. That evening, Jean, Nita and Lil got together with their new friends at Josephine's tenement. They had a great deal to talk about. Jean told them all about her day. Josephine told her that she and Rebecca worked one floor above Jean, and they could walk to work together. Then Lil and Nita told them all about their day. When Lil and Nita had gone to the Warmskuck Mill to apply for jobs, they were given a brief tour of the mill and shown the different machines like the spinning frames, power looms, carders, framing machines, finisher machines, and twisters. They were told that there were openings for spinners and weavers. They were allowed to watch both operations and then were asked which ones they were interested in. They both decided that they would like to learn to be weavers. And so began their new venture in the mill town of Exeter, New Hampshire.

After living and working in Exeter for three months, the three sisters were getting homesick for Fall River, their old friends and family. They had managed to save some money while gaining experience in their new jobs. They talked often about going back home and getting jobs there. Finally they decided it was time to head back home.

The next two weeks were very hectic. Nita and Lil submitted their resignations at the Wanskuck Mill and Jean gave her notice at Hebert Manufacturing Company. They let Mrs. Plouffe know that they would be moving out of the boarding house to return to Fall River. They thanked her for her hospitality and told her how much they enjoyed their stay. All of the boarders had been very friendly. Jean had become especially close to Maria, who was always teasing her and making her laugh. When Jean told her they were going back home, Maria gave her a big hug and told her that when she got back home, she was going to meet her true love and start a wonderful family. "Just you wait and see," she laughed and Jean blushed with embarrassment at the thought. "I hope you do too," she told Maria.

As she packed her things, Jean thought about the little mill town of Exeter, the park where she and her sisters liked to go walking, and her chats with Josephine and friends on a Sunday afternoon. It had been a pleasant three months experiencing a new independence and meeting new people. It was a community dominated by young people working in the textile mills and manufacturing shops. She was beginning to see life as a young adult embarking on a new beginning.

The girls decided to take the train back to Fall River. It wouldn't take as long as the bus trip and they would be more comfortable. Lucien offered to take them to the train station in his new car and help them with their luggage. Josephine invited Jean, Lil and Nita over for a farewell dinner. She and her roommates, Rebecca, Catherine and Suzanne prepared some French meat pies and rice pudding. The girls stopped off at the bakery and picked up some French bread still warm from the oven on their way to the tenement. When they arrived, Josephine ushered them into the kitchen. The table was set and the kitchen was filled with the delicious aroma of meat pies baking.

As they ate together, they delighted in lively conversation about their time in Exeter. They laughed about some of the things that happened at the mills and talked about their hopes and dreams, as young people often do. The economy was slowly improving and hard times were not so hard anymore. The future was full of promise for these young women.

———————————

The weather was cool and crisp and the leaves on the trees were just beginning to change colors as autumn descended on Fall River. The train pulled into the station. It was bustling with travelers and people meeting them or saying good-bye. Lil, Nita and Jean stepped off the platform with luggage in hand. They scanned the crowd looking for a familiar face. Finally, Jean spotted Uncle Arthur weaving through the crowd toward them. He hugged each of them and led them to his car. Once their luggage was stowed in the trunk, he told them how good they each looked, and how happy he was to see them. They all got into the car and Arthur drove them to Aunt Florida's home. As they drove through the Flint village, Jean felt happy to be back. After three months in Exeter, it seemed like she had been away for much longer. When they got to Aunt Florida's, Memé was watching for them through the window. As soon as she saw them, she rushed out to the porch to greet them. Aunt Florida had set out some sandwiches and pastries for them and a fresh pot of coffee. As the girls ate, Aunt Florida and Memé filled them in on the latest news and happenings since they had left. Their father's sister, Aunt Florine, had offered to rent a small apartment to the three sisters. After they had visited for a while, Uncle Arthur took them to her tenement.

The first order of business after their return was for each of them to find a job. By this time, many of the textile mills were moving down South to take advantage of newer buildings and equipment, as well as lower-wage workers. In response, the city of Fall River began to offer free mill space to manufacturers moving in. This gave rise to the rapidly growing garment industry which manufactured men's and women's clothing. With their recent training and experience in the mills of New Hampshire, Lil and Nita were able to get jobs as weavers in one of the remaining Berkshire Spinning mills and Jean took a job in Har-Lee Manufacturing where women's cotton dresses were made.

The apartment that Aunt Florine rented to the girls was on the third floor. It had a parlor with a coal stove for heat, a small kitchen and one large bedroom which the three sisters shared. They also shared household chores and expenses. Jean reconnected with her longtime friend Angie and quickly made new friends at the sewing shop. One of her new friends was named Mary DuCharme. Mary was very easy going and friendly. Another one of her new coworkers was Marcia Rossi. Marcia was quick with a joke and the three young women enjoyed each other's company.

One day, Mary was telling Jean about her boyfriend whose name was Maurice Dube. He lived up the Flint – not far from Jean, and he had an older brother named Albert. She asked Jean if she would like to meet him. She said he had a car and they could go for a ride Sunday afternoon to South Park. Jean wanted to know what Al was like and what she knew about his family. Mary said Al was a little shy, but a nice guy. She said that he worked as a taxi driver. He and Maurice had three younger brothers and two younger sisters. Jean agreed to meet him on Sunday.

Sunday was a bright and breezy autumn day. Mary knocked on the door and Jean answered. Together, they walked to the car where Maurice was waiting with his brother Al. Maurice was short and slender with sharp features and a quick smile. Al, on the other hand, was much taller than his brother but equally slender. He had softer features and a shock of black hair draped across his forehead. He gave a faint smile as he fidgeted in the driver's seat. Mary introduced Jean to Maurice and Al. Maurice greeted her warmly and Al merely gave her a little salute of acknowledgement. Mary slipped into the back seat of the car with Maurice and Jean got into the front seat with Al. As he drove to South Park, Al and Jean made small talk and tried not to look nervous. When they got to the park, they walked around for a while and then sat on a park bench to watch a baseball game that was in progress. The sun felt warm and pleasant and the four young people talked casually while Al and Jean got to know each other.

———————

Jean liked her job at Har-Lee Manufacturing. She was making twenty-six dollars a week – the most she had ever earned. She worked Monday to Friday, 7:00 AM to 4:00 PM and a half-day on Saturdays. The sewing shop was similar to the one she had worked in while in New Hampshire, although it was not as big or nearly as noisy. During morning breaks and lunch time, Mary, Marcia and Jean would get together. They would often talk about how they spent their weekend, who was going out with whom, and anything new about mutual friends. Jean had been dating Al for a couple of months and frequently went on double dates with Mary and Maurice. New Year's Eve was coming up and Al asked Jean if she would like to go to a New Year's Eve party at the Lincoln Park Ballroom in Westport. He said that Mary and Maurice and another couple he knew were going. The other couple was Frank Moss, whom Al worked with driving taxi, and his girlfriend Joan Fremont. Mary hadn't said anything to Jean about going to the ballroom until after Al had asked her to go with him. She was happy that they would welcome in the New Year together.

Jean remembered when Lil and Nita used to go out dancing at the local dance halls when Jean was too young to go with them. When she told Lil that she was going to the New Year's Eve party at the ballroom with Al, Lil offered to teach her some dance steps. They cleared an area in the parlor, put on a music record and danced around the floor. Lil was a natural on the dance floor and she taught Jean how to do the jitter-bug. When Nita came home, she joined them and showed Jean a few more dance steps. It was all a lot of fun and Jean was soon dancing to the beat of the latest music.

Jean and Mary talked about their upcoming dates as New Year's Eve approached. They had never been to a

New Year's celebration and they were very excited. Jean had heard that the ballroom at Lincoln Park was the place to be - lots of live music, dancing, noise makers, and balloons, with confetti dropping down from the chandeliers at midnight. Jean and Mary went shopping together to look for new dresses to wear to the ballroom. As they walked along Pleasant Street, they came to Delley's Women's Wear. They looked in the windows at dresses adorning the mannequins and then went inside. They each tried on several dresses. Jean picked one that was made of royal blue taffeta. It had a scoop neck and sequins strung along the neckline. The skirt was fitted at the waist then flared out. It flowed around her as she twirled around. It was the most elegant dress she had ever worn. Mary said she looked marvelous in it. Mary picked a soft velvet sheath in deep rose with a beautiful silk sash around the waist that came together in a bow. They stood side by side looking at themselves in the full length mirror. The salesgirl said they looked stunning. After purchasing their dresses, they hurried home to show them off.

New Year's Eve finally arrived. Jean and her sisters were busy getting ready for their dates. Jean looked in her drawer for her new silk stockings but she couldn't find them. She became frantic as she looked through everything. Nita asked her what she was looking for. Jean said, "I know I put my new silk stockings in this drawer and now they're gone. Have you seen them?" Nita said she saw Lil trying them on. She thought she had gotten them from Jean's drawer. Jean's face turned red as she felt a rush of anger. She looked at Lil's bed and saw the empty package from her stockings lying on top. Lil came into the room all dressed. Jean asked her where her stockings were. Lil glanced at the empty package on her bed and confessed that she had borrowed them. "I didn't think you'd mind," she said. Jean was furious. "You take them off right now. I didn't buy them for you to wear," she said. Lil was not used to her little sister standing up to her and she blushed with embarrassment. She quickly took them off and handed them to Jean. Jean finished getting dressed, all the while struggling with her feelings of anger toward her sister. "She always does things like that to me," she thought. Jean was upset and afraid that this would spoil her evening. She thought, "Now what would Bernie say?" Bernie had always been the peacemaker. Jean knew that she would tell her not to let Lil spoil her good time and then she would smile and give her a wink. That thought brought a smile to Jean's face as she looked at Bernie's picture on her bureau and felt the anger dissipate. "I will have a good time tonight," she said softly to herself.

The ballroom was aglow with sparkling streamers hanging from the ceiling. There were colored lights all along the stage. The band was playing the latest dance music. Bits of conversations floated across the room punctuated by laughter. Jean looked at Mary and smiled broadly. Mary grinned happily. Al looked tall and handsome in his new suit. He took Jean by the arm and said, "I'd like to introduce you to my friend, Frank Moss and his girlfriend, Joan Fremont. Joan – Frank, this is Jean Berthiaume and Mary Ducharme, and you already know my brother Maurice." They all shook hands, then Frank said, "Let's look for our table." When they found their table they all sat down. Frank was an energetic and talkative young man. He had an engaging sense of humor and made friends easily. He and Joan seemed to have matching personalities. She was petite and very attractive. Jean liked them both as soon as she met them.

The evening was magical. Everything was so festive. The music had everyone tapping their feet and dancing around the floor. Jean felt like Cinderella at the ball. At midnight, the balloons cascaded from the chandeliers. The colored lights started flashing along the stage and everyone cheered as they spun and blew on their noisemakers. Al looked at Jean, then, he leaned over to her and gave her a kiss. The band leader called out, "Happy New Year 1938!"

HEADLINES OF THE TIMES

THE FALL RIVER HERALD NEWS

1938

NAVY TO RETAIN TORPEDO STATION IN NEWPORT

JAP PLANES STRAFE HEAVILY POPULATED CANTON

CITY TO SEEK WPA GRANT OF MILLION DOLLARS

GARMENT WORKERS DEMAND WAGE OF $14/WEEK

GERMANS INVADE AUSTRIA; CHANSELLOR YIELDS
TO HITLER IN HOPES OF AVOIDING BLOODSHED

FIRST LADY VISITS FALL RIVER AT WPA OFFICE

HOWARD HUGHS SETS ROUND-THE-WORLD RECORD
OF LESS THAN FOUR DAYS

HAR-LEE MFG. EXPANDS IN FALL RIVER

CZECHOSLOVACIA FORCED TO SURRENDER
GERMAN SUDETENLAND TO HITLER TO AVOID WAR

HURRICANE SWEEPS CITY; AREA LEFT IN SHAMBLES
DEATH TOLL IN GREATER FALL RIVER CLIMBS TO 57

POLISH JEWS ROUNDED UP IN GERMANY; NAZIS TO
DRIVE OUT THOUSANDS

CZECHS MOBILIZE EXPECTING FURTHER GERMAN
INVASION; EUROPE ARMS FOR WAR

1938

One February evening, the weather turned very cold. Jean got out a new bag of coal and replenished the coal stove. Lil said it seemed like they were using a lot of coal, since she had opened a new bag just the day before. "You know," Nita said, "Aunt Florine was in the apartment when I came home yesterday and I asked her why she was there. She said she was just checking the windows because she felt a draft in the hallway." Later she saw Aunt Florine get a bag of coal from the third floor hall closet, which was odd since her apartment was on the first floor. This was a big concern to the girls as coal was expensive and they were all sharing expenses to save money.

A couple of weeks later, as Jean was walking home from work, the wind was blowing the snow in swirls and making it difficult for her to see where she was going. She had to tramp through two feet of snow and climb over the snow banks piled up by the snow plows at every street corner. When she finally reached her tenement, she breathed a sigh of relief. She went in and climbed the stairs to the apartment she shared with her sisters. When she got to the landing, she saw her Aunt Florine coming out of their apartment with a half-filled bag of coal. Her aunt turned around and saw her at the top of the stairs. She started to stammer, "I, ah, I was ah, just borrowing a little coal. I'm all out and it's too bad outside to go out for more." Jean looked straight at her and Aunt Florine quickly averted her eyes. "We need our coal as much as you do. Our apartment gets just as cold," she answered. Aunt Florine promised that she would replace it tomorrow, and then she lowered her head and walked past Jean and down the stairs. Jean did not know what to do. She and her sisters needed the coal but they needed the apartment too. She shook her head and went into her flat.

When Lil and Nita came home, Jean told them what had happened. They decided they would look for a new apartment right away but not say anything to their aunt until they found one. A week later, Aunt Florine had not replaced the coal she took and she said no more about it. Jean, Nita and Lil asked their friends and relatives if they knew of any apartment that was available and they checked the newspaper every night. When it was time to pay the rent, Jean went to her aunt's apartment. She opened the door but left Jean standing in the hallway. Jean gave her the rent money. Still her aunt said nothing about the coal, so Jean asked her when she would replace it. Aunt Florine said she had none to spare, but she would get some as soon as she could, and then she closed the door on Jean.

Two weeks later, Nita found an apartment with the help of a friend. The sisters went to look at it. It was on Second Street on the third floor. It was bigger than the one they had, with a kitchen, parlor, dining room and two bedrooms. They decided to take it because the rent was not much more than they were already paying their aunt. They would use the dining room as a third bedroom since there was room in the kitchen for a table and chairs. Al, Maurice and Lil's boyfriend, Joe Gendreau, helped them move. It was difficult carrying furniture up the two flights of stairs but they didn't have many pieces. They had borrowed some furniture from Aunt Florida and one of their cousins until they had enough money to buy furniture of their own.

In May of 1938, Memé (Amanda Michaud) died at the age of sixty-eight. She died of a heart attack but she had been well up until that time. Memé had been born in Quebec. She came to Fall River when she was a young woman. She married Peter Rioux and they had three daughters and three sons. Jean's mother, Rosanna was the oldest. After Peter died, Amanda took the children back to Quebec. She married a second time, to Delphis Guay and had two more sons and two more daughters. When Rosanna was a young woman, she taught in a two room country school, but the pay was very little and times were very hard. Amanda and Delphis decided to bring the family to Fall River where there were jobs in the cotton mills. Rosanna went with them.

Memé was laid out in Aunt Florida's parlor. Her many friends and relatives came to the house to attend her wake. It went on for three days. Jean, Lil and Nita took turns with their many cousins sitting up with her body each night while she was laid out in the casket. People were in and out all day long and many brought food with them to help out the family. At times there were so many people standing around talking and reminiscing that it seemed like there was a big party going on. Memé would have liked that.

110

On the second day, Bernie and Aime came from Connecticut to attend the funeral. Jean was so happy to see them that she insisted they spend the night with her, Lil and Nita. She and Lil shared a bed so that Bernie and Aime could use Jean's bedroom. When they arrived, Jean said, "Bernie, you look wonderful. How many more weeks 'til the baby is due?" Bernie told her she was due in four weeks. She and Aime had been busy getting everything ready. Jean asked if they had picked out names yet. They had been thinking about names for months and finally narrowed it down to Lorraine for a girl and Peter for a boy. That evening at the apartment, the four sisters and Aime recalled their memories of Memé. Bernie had been especially close to her after Momma died, and sought her advice while she struggled to keep the four of them together. Aime remembered the first time he met her and she warned him to be good to Bernie. She told him that he was a very handsome and charming man, but he must only have eyes for Bernie. He laughed at the thought and said he wouldn't dare look at anyone else or he was sure she would come back to haunt him.

The funeral mass was at Notre Dame d'Lourdes Church. The mass was very long and everyone was very tired by the time they got to the cemetery. The final blessing was given by Father LaFlamme. After the casket was lowered into the ground, Memé's children and grandchildren each tossed a flower on the casket.

Jean and Al became close friends with Joan and Frank from the time they all had met. They frequently went out on dates together and enjoyed each other's company. Frank was the life of the party and would have them all in stitches whenever they got together. One of their favorite places to eat was Mark You's Chinese Restaurant on Pleasant Street. Chow mein and fried rice was always a favorite. It was always served with the freshest French bread and a pot of tea. Each booth had a juke box. You could drop in a quarter and play your favorite songs. It was always lively with conversation and laughter. The owner and manager catered to the neighborhood clientele by serving fish and chips every Friday. They knew that most of the people who lived up the Flint were French Catholics and would refrain from eating meat on Fridays, as dictated by the church. There was always vinegar on the tables for the French fries and fish. After dinner they would walk down to the Strand Theater and take in a movie for twenty-five cents.

Woolworth's Five-and-Ten-Cent Store was another favorite with the best lunch counter around, especially for Jean and her childhood friend Angie on a Saturday afternoon. Sometimes they would have lunch and other times they would stop in for an ice cream soda. Something they never could afford when they were youngsters. Then there was Zeke's Restaurant run by Debe "Zeke" Assad where you could get the best hot dogs and burgers in town, topped off with the best coffee in town. In the summertime, Jean, Al, Frank, and Joan often went to Lincoln Park just over the line in Westport. They would ride on the ferris wheel, the tilt-a-whirl and the bumper cars, then wind their way through the fun house, where spooky clowns would jump out at you in the dark. There was a "dizzy" room to walk through where the floor was tilted and it was difficult to keep your equilibrium as you grabbed hold of the railings on the walls so you wouldn't fall. There was even a chute to walk through where there were two planks across the floor. They were just wide enough so that you walked across with one foot on each plank. The planks kept moving forward and backward in opposite directions from each other and a jet of air kept spurting up from the floor as the ladies passed, blowing up their skirts and dresses. The four friends would come out laughing and hanging on to each other. When they got hungry, they went over to the pavilion where clam cakes and chowder were being served. There was usually a band, a comedian or some other act going on onstage in the pavilion throughout the day. The four friends didn't have a lot of money, but they knew how to have a good time on the cheap.

On Labor Day weekend, Jean and Joan planned to go with Al and Frank to the traveling carnival that had set up in South Park. The day was sunny and warm. There was a light breeze coming off the water. Mount Hope Bay could be seen from the park in the distance as the streets sloped down to the shore. The atmosphere was festive as the park filled with people of all ages with children running through the crowd, parents calling out for them, young couples trying their luck at the game booths, and teenage boys trying to impress the girls with their skills. Al tried to win a prize for Jean at one booth by throwing darts and popping the balloons that were bobbing around in the breeze. No luck! Then Frank tried. He managed to hit every balloon, to Jean's and Joan's delight. Joan picked a teddy bear for the prize. Not to be outdone, Al tried again, this time at the shooting gallery. He hit eight out of ten targets but it wasn't enough for a prize so he tried another round. The girls cheered him on with each hit. He hit each target up to the last one. He blessed himself, took careful aim one more time and hit the target. He looked at Jean with a big grin. "What prize do you want?" he asked. Jean chose a small vase made of carnival glass. It sparkled in the sunlight, changing colors from pink to blue as the light shifted. Carnival glass was very popular then.

The two couples meandered around the booths and amusement rides saying hello to friends they met. They shared some cotton candy and popcorn they bought as they passed the food booths. Down the hill from the carnival, a band was playing at the bandstand, so they sat on the grass for a while, enjoying the music. When the music stopped, some politicians gave short speeches praising the American workers and the improving economy. A few people gathered around to listen but most of the crowd headed back to the carnival for more lively entertainment.

In the late afternoon, the couples headed for Mark You's Restaurant for some chow mein and fried rice. They ran into Lil and her boyfriend Joe as they were coming out of the restaurant. Lil and Joe had just gotten engaged and Lil eagerly showed them her engagement ring.

On the blustery autumn afternoon of September twenty-first, Jean, Mary and Marcia came out of Har-Lee Manufacturing at the end of their shift. The wind whipped around them, sending their hats airborne. Jean was able to grab Marcia's hat as it flew by. Mary chased down her own hat and grabbed Jean's in midair. They all laughed as they locked their arms together and started walking home. By the time they had all reached Mary's apartment, the sky had turned a strange yellow hue. The wind had picked up even more and small branches were being snapped off the trees and blown around. Jean was the last to reach home. She had to push with all her might to close the door against the wind. She hurried up the two flights of stairs and went into the apartment. Lil and Nita were already there, listening to the radio. The news reporter said that a hurricane was descending on the city with winds of over one hundred miles an hour and carrying torrential rains. There were reports of thirty foot waves coming up Narragansett Bay and heading for Fall River. Newscasters were warning people to stay inside away from windows which could be blown out by the wind.

By suppertime, high winds were blowing the heavy rains horizontally. The electricity was out all over the city and nearby Rhode Island. Gusts of wind shook the house and rattled the windows. The sisters wrapped themselves in blankets and huddled together in the parlor with the only light coming from an oil lamp they had lit. The wind howled all through the night as the rain pounded against the windows. Fortunately, none of them broke. Each time they dozed off, they would be awakened by the noise coming from the wind and rain and flying debris. It was a long scary night. In the morning, the wind was still blowing and the sky was still dark. The rain was slowing down. By afternoon, the wind subsided and the rain stopped. The girls ventured outside as the clouds cleared and the sun came out. It was eerily quiet as they walked down the street toward South Main Street. There were large and small tree branches everywhere and even entire trees were down. Pieces of wood, roof tiles and broken glass were all over the streets. Store windows were blown out and debris was everywhere. They looked down Columbia Street, which sloped down to Mount Hope Bay. They could see that the lower streets were flooded with several feet of water from the bay. The girls decided they should go home when they saw electrical wires dangling from the telephone poles.

When they got back home, they turned on their battery operated radio. There were reports of power outages everywhere. Winds of one hundred and twenty-one miles an hour had swept homes off their foundations all along the Rhode Island and Massachusetts coastline. Thirty foot waves swept boats into the harbor, smashing them against buildings as they were tossed onto the piers and roadways. It was later said that it was the worst storm in one hundred and fifteen years. It was several weeks before electricity was restored and people could go back to work. Some of the mills close to the water were flooded and badly damaged. Some were beyond repair. In Fall River alone there were eighty-four people killed in the storm and millions of dollars in property damage. The hurricane of 1938 proved to be an historic event. It would be talked about for generations.

116

Over the next few weeks, Lil began planning her upcoming wedding. She told Jean that Joe's sister offered to lend Lil her wedding gown and Lil wanted Jean to be her maid of honor. Joe was planning to ask Al to be one of the ushers. Jean said to Lil, "I'd love to be your maid of honor, but I really can't afford to buy a fancy dress to wear right now." Lil looked disappointed, and then she said, "You have to do this. I already asked Nita and she said she couldn't. I'm counting on you. After all, I'm going to have a big wedding and I need a maid of honor. What will the Gendreau family think?" Lil's future in-laws owned the well-known Gendreau's Furniture Store on Pleasant Street and Lil wanted to impress them. Jean felt conflicted. She wanted to do it for Lil's sake but she really couldn't afford to buy a dress because she had recently bought a bedroom set for their apartment, and she still had a few payments to make on it. She said she needed to think about it. For the next two weeks, Lil kept telling Jean that she was depending on her to say yes.

While at work, Jean told her friend Mary about her dilemma. Mary said that her sister was in a wedding last year and she hadn't worn the dress since. Maybe she would let Jean borrow it. They were about the same size and she was pretty sure it would fit Jean. She said that she would ask her and let Jean know.

Lil started talking about her wedding plans incessantly, assuming that Jean would be her maid of honor. Jean kept reminding her that she wasn't sure she could do it. By the end of the week, Mary told Jean that she spoke to her sister, and she would let Jean borrow the dress if she wanted to. On the weekend, Mary brought the dress over for Jean to try on. It was a lovely dark green taffeta slim fitting dress with an organdy skirt over the taffeta. It fit Jean beautifully. Lil said she loved it and finally Jean agreed to wear it as her maid of honor.

The wedding was scheduled for October eighteenth. Lil announced to Jean and Nita that she and Joe would be keeping the apartment, so they needed to move out. This was a shock to them both since they expected to keep the apartment, and it would be hard to find a new one that they could afford on such short notice. Lil also told them that they would have to take their own furniture out before the wedding or leave it for her and Joe. Jean told Nita that she was very upset with Lil over all of this, and there was no way she was going to leave her new bedroom set for Lil and Joe. Nita said she was upset too, especially at having to find a new apartment on such short notice. They debated whether to tell Lil that she should be the one to move out, but they knew she was already stressed out over planning the wedding and didn't want to add to it. For the next three weeks, it was a mad scramble to find a new apartment and move out before the wedding. Jean tried to keep things civil between her and Lil, but it was hard to hide her resentment. Once again, Aunt Florida saved the day by finding an apartment for Jean and Nita, and they moved in two days before the wedding. Lil had her new furniture delivered later the same day. Her new in-laws had been very generous since they owned a furniture store. They let Joe buy all the furniture at cost. Lil complained that she thought they should have given the furniture to them as a wedding gift, even though they had also agreed to pay for the reception at the Eagle Restaurant. Jean told Lil that she was expecting too much, and she should appreciate what they did do for her and Joe. Joe asked Al if he would be an usher for the wedding and he accepted. The wedding took place at Notre Dame Church. Everything went smoothly and the reception was enjoyed by many friends and relatives.

Bernie and Aime brought their four month old daughter, Lorraine, to the wedding and stayed over the weekend to visit with Jean, Nita and Aunt Florida. They each took turns playing with Lorraine, feeding her and cuddling her. Bernie said she was getting so much attention that she would surely be spoiled by the time they went home, and then she laughed and threatened to bring her back if she started crying.

Jean's friend, Joan Fremont, had her own little apartment on Robeson Street. It was a three room flat on the third floor. She had been living there for about six months. One day she told Jean that she wanted to make some new curtains for her kitchen. She had just bought a Singer sewing machine so she could learn how to sew. Jean offered to show her how to use it. "We have Singer sewing machines at the sewing shop where I work," she told Joan. They made plans to go out and buy some material on Saturday. That morning, Jean met Joan at

Woolworth's Five-and-Ten-Cents store and looked at the bolts of cloth until they found some that Joan liked for the curtains. Jean helped her figure out how much she would need to buy. Joan bought some matching thread, and they headed for Joan's apartment. It was a bright sunny day in early November and they enjoyed walking along Pleasant Street, looking in all the store windows and talking about things they liked to do. When they got to Joan's apartment, Jean showed her how to measure and cut the curtains. Next, she showed her how to thread the sewing machine and had her practice sewing straight lines on some pieces of scrap material. With Jean's help, Joan sewed each panel of cloth into curtains. After she ironed them and hung them in the windows, they both stood back to admire them. "You're a quick learner Joan," Jean complemented her friend. "Sit awhile and I'll fix us some lunch," offered Joan.

As they ate their sandwiches, they talked about Frank and Al. They talked about their futures, their hopes and dreams, marriage and children. "Do you ever talk about marriage with Frank?" Jean asked. "Yes, we've talked about it. Frank says he's been saving as much of his pay as he can, but he doesn't make much driving a taxi. Times are starting to get better though. With all the programs that President Roosevelt started, there are more jobs opening up." "I read in the paper that new businesses are coming to Fall River. Firestone Rubber and Tire brought new jobs just last year," Jean added. "Are you and Al getting serious?" asked Joan. "Well, I told him I would like to have a family and he said that he would too. Then he said, 'Let's have a little fun first,' so I guess he's not quite ready to settle down – but then he says he loves me and hopes that we will get married someday." "Maybe we'll get married at the same time," mused Joan. "It's fun to think about being married, having children and watching them grow up. It all seems so right. It's like we've finally grown up and can do whatever we want, don't you think?" Jean said. "I guess that's what it means to be coming of age." Joan smiled in reply as they daydreamed of things to come.

HEADLINES OF THE TIMES

THE FALL RIVER HERALD NEWS

1939

To Marry Next Month

Miss Jean Berthiaume

Mrs. Joseph Gendreau of Rocliffe Street, announces the engagement of her sister, Jean Berthiaume of 98 Park Street, to Albert Dube, son of Mr. and Mrs. Michael Dube of 362 Mulberry Street. The bride-elect is the daughter of the late Mr. and Mrs, James Berthiaume. The wedding will take place Feb. 18 at St. Anne's Church.

1939

Jean and Al became engaged on Christmas Day. Joan and Frank also got engaged for Christmas. They were thrilled to be planning their weddings together. They were going to be married in February. Al and Jean would wed on the eighteenth and Frank and Joan would wed one week later. Both weddings would be at St. Anne's Church on South Main Street. The two best friends went shopping together for wedding outfits. They both decided that they would rather spend their savings on furniture than on an expensive wedding gown, so they decided that they would each buy a fashionable lady's suit. They went to Mcquirr's Department Store on South Main Street. They also went to Delley's Women's Wear and Annette's Dress Shop. This was one time when Jean thoroughly enjoyed shopping for clothes, knowing that she could afford to buy something she really liked. The thought of it being for her wedding made it even more exhilarating. Joan was enjoying herself as much as Jean. Together, they tried on different suits, paired them with blouses, hats, gloves and shoes, critiqued each outfit and felt like fashion models. In the end, Jean chose a dark blue tailored wool suit that accentuated her slim figure. She picked out a matching blue velvet hat with an upward shaped brim and a veil that fell almost to her shoulders. Her blouse was made of white silk with soft pleats along the shoulder and a lace collar. She completed the outfit with white gloves and dark blue pumps. She looked very elegant.

Jean and Al went to St. Anne's Church to arrange for the wedding. They would be having a small, intimate wedding with family members and a few close friends. Jean asked Al who he would want for his best man. Jean had asked her sister Nita to be her maid of honor so Al asked her what she thought of his asking Nita's boyfriend, Stanley Sekunda. "Well, from what Nita tells me, they will probably be the next to get married, so I guess that would be a good choice. I'm sure Nita would like that." "Why don't we invite them out to dinner and I can ask him then?" Al said, and so they did. When Al asked him, Stanley said that he would be happy to be their best man.

Aunt Florida said they could have the reception at her house. She offered to commandeer all the aunts and cousins to help her prepare the food. All Jean would need to do was provide the wedding cake. Jean told Aunt Florida that she was very grateful for her help. She said that she could always count on her aunt and gave her a big hug and a kiss. Aunt Florida gave her a big smile and said, "I wish your mother could be here. She would be so proud of you."

The marriage of Jean and Al brought an end to their childhood years. As young adults, they embarked on a new life together. They raised a son and a daughter. They were married for fifty-five years when Al died at the age of seventy-seven. They had five grandsons, a great-grandson, and two great-granddaughters. Jean was a widow for sixteen more years and died at the age of ninety-one. The world had changed in many ways during Jean's lifetime. Growing up during the Great Depression had a significant influence on her experiences. Her childhood had taught her how to cope with difficult times and significant losses. She learned to rely on her own strengths and resources. Through her own struggles, she resolved to make a better life for herself and her family. Our earliest experiences tend to have the greatest influence on our development. The times we grow up in often determine those experiences. How our family members respond to them, influence us in many ways and in many ways we influence the next generation. There is a thread that connects us from generation to generation, from parent to child, from grandparent to grandchild. It teaches us that family matters.

Jean Berthiaume and Albert Dube
Married
June 18, 1939

29686239R00078

Made in the USA
Charleston, SC
20 May 2014